Uncoverings
1982

Volume 3 of the Research Papers of the American Quilt Study Group

edited by Sally Garoutte

Published by the American Quilt Study Group
660 Mission Street, Suite 400
San Francisco CA 94105-4007
Manufactured in the United States

Second printing 1993
ISBN 1-877859-05-2
ISSN 0227-0628
Library of Congress catalog card number: 81-649486

Cover photo: *Scrap Quilt (1930s)*
made by Elva Wilson
of Clifty Community, Tennessee
Owner: Edna Gossage
Photo courtesy of Merikay Waldvogel

This volume is supported by a generous donation from
Winifred Sharp Reddall,
a founding member of American Quilt Study Group

Contents

Foreword

Research into the history of American quilts and their makers continues at an incessant pace, to which this third volume of UNCOVERINGS attests. The outstanding variety of subjects—from an intimate insight into one needleworker's productive life and work to a highly focused examination of a single quilt's design elements—illustrates the fascinating complexity of the cultural phenomenon called "quiltmaking." It is exciting!

UNCOVERINGS provides the vehicle to disseminate the details of new research discoveries. Each revelation, no matter how small, triggers fresh challenges for further findings. The more we learn of the people, their needs and motivations as expressed through one artifact, the quilt, the better we are able to understand ourselves and our future.

It is with a great deal of satisfaction and pride that the American Quilt Study Group presents the ten research papers that follow.

Some Aspects of an 1809 Quilt

Tandy Hersh

In 1968 the Smithsonian Institution offered a course entitled "Textiles" for their Associates Program. Rita Adrosko, Doris Bowman and Gladys Cooper, the ABC's of the Division of Textiles at that time, lectured on facets of tapestry, linens, the spinning wheel, coverlets, flags, quilts, the sewing machine, and other subjects. They used the finest quality examples from the Smithsonian's collection to illustrate the lectures. In the session on quilts, they showed us a glazed wool quilt made in Vermont in the late 18th century, with the finish still as shiny as today's glazed chintz. Thanks to that course and that particular quilt, I found the subject of this paper.

I live in Carlisle, Pennsylvania, in the Cumberland Valley, where the first Scotch-Irish settler came in 1725. By 1731, four hundred Scotch-Irish families had settled in the area and began a significant influx in that decade, which resulted in a preponderance of the population at the time of the American Revolution.[1] The descendants of one of these families, the McCullochs, sold their household goods and farm equipment at an auction in 1980. Discarded and pushed back into a corner was a damaged quilt folded with the backing side out. On examination it proved to be the same type material as that in the Smithsonian quilt. One of my friends tells me I am a textile salvager instead of a textile collector, and I think she is correct. Rather than search for perfect items only, I look for textiles which have come apart, as they provide an opportunity to study construction techniques. It bothers me that these frayed things, created with such effort in an earlier time, have outlived the purpose for which they were made, so the torn, incomplete, faded, and repaired fabrics become my favorite things, and afford me a chance to learn from them. The quilt was only a study piece the day of the auction, and

Martha Tandy Hersh, who comes from a long line of Kentucky quilters, is a textile researcher and lover of old fabrics. Her address is: Box 458, AWC, Carlisle Barracks, PA 17013.

though I have tried to make it seem otherwise, that is, a silk purse out of a sow's ear, it is still a study piece rather than a show piece.

My purpose in this paper is to present a "micro" analysis of this quilt. Sally Garoutte's paper "Early Colonial Quilts in a Bedding Context" in UNCOVERINGS 1980 was a "macro" analysis in comparison, the study of a large number of quilts mentioned in wills and inventories in given areas and times.[2] I will describe and analyze one glazed wool quilt with the date September 13, 1809, and initials MRMc quilted along one edge, and compare it with similar quilts to determine what can be learned by this approach.

The quilt measures eighty inches wide and ninety-five inches long. It weighs seven and one-half pounds, and is made of three layers of wool. The decorative top has sixty ten-inch squares set as diamonds. There are twenty-two equal size triangles around the edges and a smaller triangle at two corners. The pattern of the top is achieved by alternating solid watermelon pink and black squares. The backing is a dull apricot wool material, and the filling is wool fibers. The worn aspect is that all of the black glazed wool squares, fifty percent of the quilt top, have disintegrated, the wool backing has extensive edge damage, the filling shows through, and, surely, we may regard it as another salvaged textile.

In the spirit of this detailed study of one quilt we will first analyze the materials from which it was made, and then consider the construction process. The primary focus of our study, however, will be the quilting itself, especially the design elements and how they are combined. Following this, we will compare this quilt with others of its type, and finally draw some conclusions.

Analysis of the Materials

Imported wool textiles were important furnishings in colonial homes. By the middle of the 18th century, moreen, camlet, harrateen, cheyney, calamanco, and other wool fabrics were listed in inventories of estates in America. The more affluent families used these materials for bed hangings and coverings, upholstery, curtains and clothing.[3] Some of these expensive fabrics were made in America, but the majority came from England and France. This lightweight wool cloth had plain, glazed and watered surfaces, damask-like designs permanently embossed in it by heat or pressure, and was dyed in beautiful colors. The colored photographs in

Fig. 1. Quilting designs, all-wool quilt, Pennsylvania, maker unknown. "September 13, 1809—MRMc" in the quilting. Author's drawing. Hersh collection.

AMERICAN QUILTS AND COVERLETS by Bishop and Safford,[4] and WOMAN'S DAY BOOK OF AMERICAN NEEDLEWORK by Rose Wilder Lane[5] will give an idea of the color range. Flowers, stripes, varying size weft threads for texture, different weave structures, plus the fact that it was relatively fire retardant, made wool very desirable as a furnishing fabric.[6]

It is difficult to give names and processes of manufacture to specific wool fabrics made in the 18th century because of lack of documentation at the time of production. Many definitions of fabric names were written in the late 19th century, and are not necessarily accurate for 18th century processes, so I will use the larger classification of "glazed wool" when I refer to the top. Glazing was accomplished by applying heat or pressure on fabrics after preparing its surface with a solution. Heat or friction removed fuzzy short hairs and a smooth light-reflecting cloth resulted. Calamanco seems to be the current name most often associated with glazed wool. Hazel E. Cummin's article "Calamanco" in THE MAGAZINE ANTIQUES quotes from early English and French publications describing wool fabrics. The characteristics of calamanco evoke adjectives like crisp, lightweight, glossy, plain, solid, beautiful, clear colors, and all of these seem to describe the material in this 1809 quilt.[7] There is one problem, however, in referring to this cloth as calamanco since the 18th century French source describes the weave structure of calamanco as a five harness satin weave. The weave structure of our quilt is plain weave. One interesting small discovery is somewhat gratifying on this point. Our quiltmaker used two scraps of black satin weave material. One is a corner triangle, and the other piece would never have been seen if the black material of one block had not deteriorated, exposing a hidden patch of reinforcement done in reverse applique. The patch is sewn with large linen stitches on the hidden underside, and almost invisible stitches on the top.

The individual threads in the glazed wool top are finely spun, and there are forty-eight threads per inch in both warp and weft. The threads are not plyed, but are called singles, and, except as noted above, are woven in a balanced plain weave. There are three colors: black, watermelon pink, and shrimp. The shrimp was used to complete the top when the pink scraps ran out, and examination of hidden folds demonstrates these colors have not changed and the material is well preserved. The black pieces have changed to a dark black-green color, and their poor condition could be the result of corrosive black dyes, or from the black being a recycled material in 1809. Some squares are made of two smaller pieces seamed together to make the ten-inch square. Very likely all of this material was commercially made and was not the product of a single artisan. A final observation on the satin weave piece should note two tan colored threads in the selvage. Ruth McKendry in TRADITIONAL QUILTS AND BED COVERINGS reports three blue selvage threads appear in cotton exported from England between 1774 and 1811.[8] The filling is a thin layer of carded wool fibers spread between the top and back.

The dull apricot colored backing appears to have been used, possibly as a blanket made of three lengths seamed together, before it was cut into seven pieces to fit the top of the quilt. It is singles, wool, but has only twenty-eight warp threads and thirty-two weft threads per inch, heavier individual threads than those in the top, and is a two over two twill weave. It is handspun, z twist, and hand woven, with the diagonal line of the twill erratic, indicating the uneven beat of a nonprofessional weaver. It too has its story to tell. Areas are darned, a neat repair patch was made before it was quilted, and there is an inch and three-quarters band of a different weave in it. Perhaps the weaver used a different treadling to spread the warp as she began to weave. This band was woven with one twill shot followed by one plain weave shot, instead of four successive twill shots. This material after processing measured thirty-four and one-half inches wide, a width typical of seamed blankets of the period.

Construction

The Scotch-Irish lady joined the materials with linen, wool, and cotton threads. All squares have been seamed together with two-ply unbleached linen thread, in back stitch, with eight to nine stitches per inch, of course by hand. (The sewing machine was patented thirty-seven years later.) The seam allowances vary, but three-eighths inch is an average. The edges of the top are folded down one-half inch toward the back. The back edges are folded down one-half inch toward the front, and these two folded edges are sewn together with two straight rows of quilting. This was an effective finish, because on the two sides where the material remained well preserved, the edges are intact. All of the quilting threads are three-ply wool, black thread on black squares, rusty red thread on pink squares and there is an average of five stitches per inch. The three-ply, rose color cotton thread was used to patch and darn the backing, and overcast the four smaller backing pieces together. Two-ply

wool, the same color as the backing fabric, was used to overcast the
longest seam between the two largest pieces.

Design Elements

The bold, dominant design feature in the quilt is the alternating,
contrasting colored squares set in a diamond pattern. It is a design
used in decorating 18th century floors and floorcloths as illustrated
in Rodris Roth's FLOOR COVERINGS IN 18TH CENTURY
AMERICA.[9] These bold contrasts point up the fact that the quilt
is not balanced and has no center square in either direction.

The recessive feature, one that gives texture and subtle light
changes, is the quilting. Because the quilting threads match the
fabric, the designs do not stand out as they would if the threads were
contrasting. Black on black, even viewed closely, is hard to see.
Study of these quilting designs in the individual squares demonstrates what all quilters know, that is, the combination of a few
simple shapes, when repeated in an orderly manner, compound, and
become the basis of all quilting. Figure 1, a drawing of the whole
quilt, shows what our quilter created with the circle, intersecting
circle, the half circle, straight lines, and the spiral form.

This drawing attempts to copy designs, errors, and irregularities
faithfully. The quilter took each ten-inch square as a separate area
unrelated to the next and, using curved and straight lines, composed
a unique design, and then moved to the next square for a new composition. She did duplicate within the sixty blocks many times, but
only once do two identical blocks lie adjacent to each other so you
can see the effect of the completion of intersecting circles. There is a
combination of free-drawn patterns and the use of guides, such as an
eight-inch plate for the large circle and a template for the eight- and
twelve-petaled roses. All the other designs are unmeasured and not
uniform.

In Figure 2, row 1 shows the simple fundamental shapes from
which all the patterns developed. Row 2 shows two squares with
examples of background or overall patterns: cross hatching and
shells. The next line shows the six corner patterns the quilter used:
two fans, concentric quarter-circles, a single quarter-circle, diagonal
lines, and one in which all ribs of a fan emanate from a point on the
long side of a triangle.

Fig. 2. Basic shapes included in the quilting designs. Author's drawing.

In the center of many blocks she drew a large circle and put a twelve-petal rose, spiral shapes, and interlocking circles inside, sometimes putting scallops around the edge, sometimes not. Other times she used scallops without a large circle. Midway between corners on the edge of various squares she made two concentric arcs, three shells, four petals or two nested "L" shaped lines. Hearts developed from two ribs of the fan. These are geometric designs. There are no large scale squares, no vines, grapes, plumes, feathers, tendrils, or designs based in nature.

You can see the variety of combinations of patterns, the lack of orderly placement of the patterns and the mistakes, but being quilters and people who study quilts, you can also see the potential from any single block pattern to its compounding, and thus to its becoming the overall quilting design for a single quilt. I was so busy finding the date block after I got home from the auction and trying to research the settlement of the area and the maker by searching deeds, genealogies and cemetery records, that I didn't study the quilt, and missed the point that is obvious now, but that my husband had to suggest. The quilt is indeed a sampler of quilting designs which could be referred to for subsequent use.

My interest then shifted to the source of the designs. Is it possible that the rural area of Cumberland County with the McCrae, McCulloch, McKinney, McMeans, McMurray, McCormick, McKeon, and other Scotch-Irish familes was so insular that in 1809 these ladies were still using the designs the families brought here in the 1730s? Averil Colby's book QUILTING, written in England with much of the research done in the British Isles, has cross hatching, shells, fans, roses with scalloped petals, concentric circles, intersecting circles, even the idea of spirals left and right off of a vertical line, in diagram form in Chapter 4. Photographs of 18th century articles on which these designs were quilted are in Chapter 8.[10] I have not taken the next step to research other cultural backgrounds of quilting, so I can't say with confidence that the design elements of our quilt are definitely from the British Isles, but certainly there is an affinity.

Comparisons

We have looked at the detailed features of this quilt, and now should consider where it fits in the chronology of American quilts by asking some questions. What was its forerunner? The glazed wool whole-cloth quilt was an earlier bed cover and often more elegant. Widths of one solid color wool material were seamed together, interlined, and backed. Using this full top as a single large square, designs of natural forms such as pineapples, palm leaves, grapes and vines, flowers, and feathers were arranged in mirror image in an overall design. The quilting was the only design element and close rows of diagonal groundwork made the intricate pattern stand out in relief.

Is this 1809 square-set-as-diamonds quilt one of a kind? No. The Smithsonian has such a quilt made by Lucy Adler in New Hampshire with the same design and colors, but it employs different naturalisitic, rather than geometric, quilting in every square.[11]

Did embroidered designs influence these quilting designs? Plain weave blankets were woven and then marked off into squares, and large checks were woven into blankets, both creating plain squares in which wool embroidery was worked, in the same period as this quilt. You find the fundamentals of lines, curves, intersecting circles, but the designs seem to be based in natural forms rather than geometric forms, and are more complex. The embroidered blankets do have the sampler variation idea rather than one repetitive design.[12] The picture in Susan Burrows Swan's book PLAIN AND FANCY shows wool embroidery on wool squares set as diamonds. One design is made of circular shapes left and right of a principle vertical line.[13]

Are there other quilts conceived with a sampler idea? The "album" or "friendship" quilt, made twenty to thirty years later, often appeared to be a sampler of design blocks. However, the purpose of demonstrating the individuality of each friend's effort seems quite different from the design experimentation on our quilt.

Conclusions

You realize by now that this is not an extraordinary quilt, that it followed the early American practice of saving all fabric for future use and of using what was at hand, that its maker was an average needlewoman, that much of the quilting was free hand, that it was not planned as a work of art, that it is rural and not high style, that it recorded designs for future references, and that it could possibly stem from a Scotch-Irish heritage.

I have included 18th century with the early 19th century comparisons because of the fabric, and also because of the lag in the time when styles of furniture, decorative arts, and clothing were popular in an urban area, and when those same styles were interpreted in a sparsely populated area.

For me, this study quilt, despite its worn appearance, has provided an incentive to read sources unknown to me before, and to reread familiar works on weaving, quilting, and textiles in general. It has stimulated a need for me to visit curators and staff members at the Smithsonian Institution, Winterthur Museum, William Penn Museum, and the Metropolitan Museum of Art. It has given me an excuse to talk with my friends in the textile field, and courage to visit some outstanding antique dealers in New York. Finally, it demonstrates the value of retaining damaged fabrics in their entirety for detailed examination, an approach which provides for another perspective for quilt study.

Notes and References

1. Wayland F. Dunaway, THE SCOTCH-IRISH OF COLONIAL PENNSYLVANIA, Genealogical Publishing Co., Inc., Baltimore, 1979, pp. 59–61.
2. Sally Garoutte, "Early Colonial Quilts in a Bedding Context" in UNCOVERINGS 1980, American Quilt Study Group, Mill Valley, California, 1981.
3. Anna Brightman, "Woolen Window Curtains," THE MAGAZINE ANTIQUES, Vol. 86, No. 6, (December 1964), pp. 722–727.
4. Carleton L. Safford and Robert Bishop, AMERICA'S QUILTS AND COVERLETS, Weathervane Books, New York, 1974, pp. 28–37.
5. Rose Wilder Lane, WOMAN'S DAY BOOK OF AMERICAN NEEDLEWORK, Simon and Schuster, New York, 1963, pp. 116–117.
6. Anna Brightman, p. 725.
7. Hazel E. Cummin, "Calamanco" THE MAGAZINE ANTIQUES, Vol. 39, No. 4 (April 1941), pp. 182–184.
8. Ruth McKendry, TRADITIONAL QUILTS AND BED COVERINGS, Van Nostrand Reinhold, 1979.
9. Rodris Roth, FLOOR COVERINGS IN 18TH CENTURY AMERICA, Smithsonian Press, Washington, D.C., 1967), p. 14.
10. Averil Colby, QUILTING, Batsford, London, 1972, Chapters 4 and 8.
11. Quilt 74-4979, Division of Textiles, Smithsonian Institution.
12. Quilt 65 203, Newark Museum, Newark, New Jersey.
13. Susan Burrows Swan, PLAIN AND FANCY, Holt, Rinehart and Winston, New York, 1977. p. 200.

Cuna Molas: The Geometry of Background Fill

Bertha B. Brown

The Cuna Indians, also known as the San Blas Indians, occupy the Archipelago de Las Mulatas made up of a string of more than three hundred islands which lie off the northeastern coast of the Republic of Panama. Here, against a tropical setting of turquoise seas, coral islands, white sandy beaches, and coconut palms, some twenty thousand Cuna live in crowded conditions on the larger islands lying nearest the mainland.

One of Panama's three indigenous Indian cultures, the Cuna were well-established in Panama's interior upon the arrival of the Spaniards, and Cuna villages are still found along the rivers of Panama's Bayano region. It is thought by many scholars of Panamanian history that the San Blas Cuna were originally river people who gravitated to the islands to escape Spanish persecution. Whatever the reason, the islands provided an ideal environment for growing the coconuts on which their economy has come to be based, and gave them the isolation from non-Cuna people which they found so desireable.

The Cuna fostered their insular society and until well into the twentieth century they entertained a non-violent hostility towards strangers. Today, the Cuna continue to protect their racial purity and retain many traditional customs and beliefs, even while strangers of various persuasions are visitors on their islands and acculturation goes on apace.

In order to maintain communities, occupied islands must be near enough to the mainland so that daily trips may be made by boat. On the mainland the men farm small plots of land, and the women obtain fresh water from mainland rivers to take to the islands, wash

Bertha B. Brown is an avid anthropologist and bird-watcher who lived in Panama for more than thirty years. Her address is: Box 405, Carmel Valley, CA 93924.

clothes, bathe, and enjoy a social hour with friends. Much of Cuna livelihood is obtained from the sea, and Cuna men often sail on foreign vessels.

Cuna society is matriarchial so that many traditions, customs and ceremonies center about the women. Upon marriage, the bride-groom will live with, and work for, the bride's family, and although the eldest male is the head of the household, women enjoy much prestige and authority.

Cuna men wear rather ordinary western-style clothing, but the dress of Cuna women is exceedingly colorful and the pride of Cuna culture. They also wear golden nose rings and necklaces made of trade beads or fish, animal and bird bones. Their wrists and ankles are bound tightly with strings of colored beads to form interesting designs with the purpose of keeping this portion of their limbs ele-gantly slender. A hand-sewn, short-sleeved blouse which the Cuna call mola, decorated with complicated designs, along with a sarong-like skirt and a yellow and red bandana covering their short-cropped hair, completes their everyday wearing apparel. On festive occasions they may wear large, round gold ear plates, a number of gold finger rings, and gold necklaces. Red paint on the cheeks, and a black line down the center of the nose are added for beauty's sake.

It is the blouse, however, for which the Cuna are best known, an item which may take Cuna women six to eight weeks of leisure time to complete, and which has earned them a well-deserved niche in the annals of needlework. In an article on molas, art critic John Canaday observed that:

> ...the panels which they create...are brilliant artifacts at the very least, or at a higher level are folk art of a superior kind... and are very often works of fine art...[1]

The panels to which Mr. Canaday refers are the front and back panels of the Cuna blouse which are made of two or three layers of colored cotton cloth, averaging 14 x 18 inches in size. The first step involves the basting together of two layers of differently colored cloth. The outline of a preconceived design is then cut from the second layer, leaving a silhouette of the desired motif. The rough edges of the second layer are tucked under and stitched to the bottom layer, a technique often referred to as reverse applique. At this point, should the panel be completed, a two-color mola has been produced. It is more likely, however, that a third layer will now be added, the design cut out in the same fashion as the second layer, the edges again turned under and stitched down, this time leaving a narrow border of the second color framing the silhouette. The motif now can be appliqued in the area prepared for it and, depending upon its complexity, it will be completed with additional applique, inlays, inserts and other needlework embellishments. In a good mola, there will be little or no evidence of the stitching except on the reverse side of the panel where it is likely to approach machine-like perfection.

Having completed the primary motif, the Cuna needlewoman will turn her attention to the empty space surrounding the design. Here she will follow the example of many other primitive people who, in art, often avoid empty space. This is usually accomplished by introducing subordinate elements to fill those areas left blank by the motif, or by so arranging the motif that it covers the entire area which is to be decorated. Among the Cuna, space fillers are the rule, certainly in pictorial molas, but even in those abstract and geometric motifs which may occasionally cover the entire panel, there is usually some evidence of a filling pattern. It is often in the background fill that the consummate skill of the master needlewoman will appear, and the discipline of the dedicated individual becomes most apparent in the fine detail accorded to tedious and time-consuming fill elements. Cuna women resort to the use of a wide variety of shapes and forms for background fill, and the manipulation of color to achieve effects which are quite sophisticated.

The simplest and most common of the space fillers used in Cuna needlework is the vertical slot (Figure 1). It, along with the other types of space fillers, is also frequently incorporated as an element of design in the primary motif where it may serve as a feature of the motif, or serve the purpose of space filler. It may be rounded at both ends, or rectangular in shape. In both instances, the slots are cut out of the top piece of material to reveal inserts of plain colored cloth or printed material which have been introduced underneath the top layer to provide color variety. The edges of the slots are tucked under and stitched down in the same fashion as the second and top layers of the panel.

Fig. 1. An example of well-executed vertical slots.

In a variation of vertical slot fill, the inserts are replaced with varying lengths of colored strips which are sewn horizontally to empty spaces of the second layer of the panel with colors alternating both horizontally and vertically (Figure 2). Upon completion of this technique, several strips of color appear in the slot, rather than the single color or the printed pattern of an insert. In another, and even more complicated version, horizontal slots are cut into the second layer of cloth prior to adding the horizontal strips, thus adding the color of the bottom layer of the panel to an already dazzling array. Occasionally, striped or printed material may be substituted for handwork in background fill and may lead to unusual effects. Background fill made in this fashion tends to mask the motif, making it difficult to recognize.

Dots are a particularly effective, but time-consuming, form of fill (Figure 3). Here, too, inserts of colored and printed materials are stitched to the second layer, with the dots cut out of the top layer and stitched down. Artfully used, they provide a quite magnificent

Fig. 2. Vertical slots with strips of vari-colored cloth sewn to second layer for increased color.

backdrop of glowing color for the dominant motif. In an excellent panel, there may be more than twelve hundred dots, averaging 1/8″ in diameter.

The triangle is another type of fill likely to be used by the better seamstresses. Occasionally, the first triangle is cut out of the second layer to reveal the color of the last layer, and the final triangle is cut out of, and finished, on the top layer. In another technique, the triangle is cut out of the top layer only and color variation achieved by appliqueing one or two smaller triangles inside the first triangle. Further variety is sometimes attained by notching the final triangle into a "V" shape. Inserts usually are not used with this form of fill. In an especially good panel, the triangles will be closely fitted together into the empty space, and they will be of uniform size and well-shaped.

Lozenges, or diamonds (Figure 4), are also one of the finer types of fill and are produced by cutting out and stitching, rather than the

Fig. 3. A striking example of background fill produced solely by dots.

process of applique. Here, too, color variation may be attained through the use of inserts.

Words, names and phrases sometimes are part of the primary motif, but at other times appear as background fill. They most often appear in subjects that are exotic to Cuna culture. Often the Cuna seamstress responds to the visual quality of the printing she is copying rather than to any symbolical meaning that she may recognize. As a result, the letters may appear upside down, reversed, placed in the wrong order or dropped completely. Then, perhaps as a warning to the unwary, and to emphasize that generalities must be approached with caution in any discussion of Cuna art, a legend of some length and complexity will be reproduced perfectly.

A whole catalog of shapes and geometric forms in sizes ranging from small to large commonly serve the Cuna as space fillers. These include crosses, four and five-pointed stars, swastikas, zig-zags, Cuna-manufactured rick-rack, esses, ems, zees, and others too

Fig. 4. Both dots and lozenges used as fill. Color varied by inserts stitched to the second layer.

numerous to describe. Many are geometric elements (Figure 5) and running rectilinear or curvilinear patterns which are the products of the individual needlewoman's imagination. An element often figuring in background fill, especially in pictorial molas, is that of diminutive silhouettes of a major element of the motif, or several smaller elements related in some fashion to the motif theme. Perhaps most common of all is the custom of utilizing several of the types of fill described in one mola.

Abstract and geometric design molas on the whole tend not to abound in the infinite variety of space fillers so typical of pictorial molas. Often, the design is so ordered that background fill appears as an integral part of the central motif (Figure 6), a generality to which there are many exceptions.

In producing molas, Cuna women employ the color range to its fullest extent, a fact which applies as much to the background fill as

Fig. 5. Geometric elements as fill. The rectilinear shapes contrast with the
curved lines of the motif.

it does to the dominant motif. When new, the colors are often bril-
liant and explosive, since there is no hesitation in putting together
the brightest of primary colors, and using them in all hues and
shades. A sensation of dizziness may be created by the use of a green
top layer producing a design of whirligigs against a red background;
or an orange and purple maze may seem to be in motion. Color is
primarily decorative, rather than naturalistic, and may reflect the
needlewoman's desire to place utilitarian or familiar objects in a different and more exciting context. The use of color in background fill
is also a convention that prevents monotony. And while the inten-
sity of colors in a new mola may seem garish to the mola novice, the
frequent washing by Cuna owners radically alters the character of
the mola and softens the colors, giving them new complexity and
range.

Background fill is an integral part of the mola-making process.

Fig. 6. A continuous line pattern eliminates the need for background fill.

All of the fill elements now utilized may be found in older molas in one form or another. Nevertheless, changes seem to have occurred in fill quality, and it is tempting, but risky, to state that on the whole it has improved. Certainly the art of mola-making has not remained static and Cuna women have complete freedom in utilizing design motifs and background fill as they wish, as opposed to cultures in which art styles are more traditional. Among the Cuna, no motif is seen in precisely the same fashion by any two needlewomen, nor is a particular type of fill always used with the same subject matter.

A question arises. Does background fill fulfill a basic need? Is there a necessity for such a device, whether it be in molas, or in more sophisticated forms of art? Perhaps it would be informative to look at the world around us.

Consider a clear, blue sky meeting an empty, calm sea at the horizon. Think of yourself as the only sign of life on a flat, treeless seashore. Nature at this moment is lonely, monotonous and not very attractive. Now, against the horizon paint in a ridge of wooded mountains. There, at the edge of the shore, sketch in rocky ledges which have been worn down by waves, wind and time. Notice how the character of the sandy beach changes with the addition of pebbles of varying size, as well as sea shells left by waves. Add clouds, their shapes and colors in a state of constant change, moving across the sky as a playful breeze gradually becomes a more purposeful wind. Whitecaps appear, giving texture to the smooth water. Pelicans and gulls dip, glide, soar; crabs scuttle along the shore; the wooded hillsides are in motion as treetops sway with the wind. Suddenly an almost blank canvas has come alive. It has been transformed by background fill.

Imagine a newly-completed house in which no one is yet living, a house without character or life. The walls need paintings, hangings and other decorative objects. The floors need rugs to complement the furniture. Curtains will further serve to relieve the starkness of the bare walls, as well as framing the view outside the house. It is clear that this house will require a great variety of background fill to relieve its primarily utilitarian nature and satisfy the esthetic needs which are so integral a part of the human condition.

When an artist uses space on a canvas, or a composer writes a symphony, or an interior decorator looks at blank walls, or a Cuna woman starts putting together rectangles of cloth, all are faced with the common problem of empty space. The technique that will be used in filling the space is a problem that each of these individuals must solve to his own satisfaction. In the mola, the pictorial design, no matter how intricate and colorful, is stark and uninteresting when presented against a background of plain, unadorned cloth. Three moths spread out over a rectangle of material only emphasize the space that is empty. The mola requires the background fill, perhaps more so than some other forms of art.

Filling space in a symmetrical or balanced fashion is a function related to geometry. A design may be perceived at an intellectual level, or sensed at an intuitive or subconscious level. In the first instance, the design or geometrical elements can, perhaps, be reduced to an intelligent formula. This, however, is not necessarily successful art or design, since the formula cannot take into account the skill and flair of artist or designer. Rather the successful use of geometric elements involves physical response to intuitive or sub-conscious logic which results in a pleasing combination of forms, which may be square, rectangular, circular, triangular, elliptical or free form, the arrangement of which, in this instance, will serve as the basis of background fill. A variety of geometric shapes in inter-play is one of the chief means of creating good design quality. The skilled Cuna needlewoman may well think in design terms, though she may not find it possible to verbalize them. The artistic needle-woman understands the need to maintain symmetry in her design, yet this may be more apparent than real. Examination may reveal that the design is balanced, giving the illusion of symmetry, and this illusion will be carefully maintained. Small elements can be fitted nicely both into large and small spaces. Large elements fitted too closely together may hide the motif regardless of the amount of space available. A variety of highly differentiated elements may avoid monotony, but the motif may become just one more item of back-ground fill.

Among the Cuna Indians, molas were originally made only for utilitarian purposes, and for the most part this remains true today, for the mola has come to be regarded as art only in the relatively recent past. With the Cuna, however, art cannot be considered a profession which is separated from other duties. Mola-making is a part of the Cuna woman's life cycle, a function which every woman performs, beginning in childhood. With molas playing an ever-increasing role in Cuna society, however, it is likely that most Cuna women strive for artistic quality in their work. But even those who fail to achieve art will not be closed out since they must produce molas for their own use, and rarely is a mola so poor that there is no demand for it in the marketplace.

The matriarchal role of Cuna women seems to have created an environment in which creative independence and artistic ability thrive as illustrated by the best of Cuna needlework. It can be hoped that the proud Cuna men will continue to protect and nurture their women, while encouraging them to continue this fascinating Cuna tradition.

Notes and References

1. New York Times, December 28, 1968, p. D-25.

Bibliography

Biesanz, John and Mavis. THE PEOPLE OF PANAMA, Columbia University Press, New York, 1955.

Canaday, John. "All About Cuna Molas," NEW YORK TIMES,December 29, 1968, p. D-25.

_____. "Mea Culpa On The Molas, Cuerpo De Paz!" NEW YORK TIMES, August 8, 1971, p. D-17.

Carles, Ruben Dario. SAN BLAS, TIERRA DE LOS CUNAS, Editora Humanidad, S.A., Panama, 1965.

Chaves, Enrique and Angermuller, Linnea. ABOUT MOLAS, Panama Canal Press, Panama, for Isthmian Anthropology Society, Florida State University, 1969.

Corin, Georgia. "All About Molas," PANAMA CANAL REVIEW, August, 1970, pp. 22-24.

Keeler, Clyde E. CUNA INDIAN ART, Exposition Press, New York, 1969.

McAndrews, Anita. CUNA COSMOLOGY, Three Continents Press, Washington, D.C., 1978.

Mahoney, Lawrence. "Moving In On The Mola," THE MIAMI HERALD, TROPIC MAGAZINE, April 13, 1972, pp. 40-41.

Parker, Ann and Neal, Avon. MOLAS, FOLK ART OF THE CUNA INDIAN, Clarkson N. Potter, Inc., New York, 1977.

Sauer, Carl Ortwin. THE EARLY SPANISH MAIN, University of California Press, Berkeley, 1966.

Wafer, Lionel. A NEW VOYAGE AND DESCRIPTION OF THE ISTHMUS OF AMERICA, 1699, Ed. by George Parker Winship, Cleveland, Ohio, 1903.

Nine Related Quilts of Mecklenburg County, North Carolina, 1800-1840

Ellen F. Eanes

Before the American Revolution, the Scotch-Irish, called Ulstermen, left Pennsylvania and Maryland and came down the great Wagon Road to the Piedmont area of the Carolinas. This area lies between the mountain region to the west and the coastal plain to the east. Mecklenburg County lies in the Piedmont and shares a southern border with the state of South Carolina. The county was laid out in 1775 in what was in every sense the frontier (Figure 1).

These Ulstermen had been persecuted by the English in Ireland. They believed in freedom of religion and government, along with freedom of religion *from* government. The predominant religion they brought to this area was Presbyterianism, led by the fiery preacher, Alexander Craighead. He formed the churches at Rocky River and Sugar Creek. Soon others were established at Hopewell, Centre, Poplar Tent, Providence and Steele Creek. All were in what was then Mecklenburg County.

Settlers in Charlotte, the major city of Mecklenburg County, raised a crude log cabin courthouse and the town was incorporated in 1768. On May 19, 1775, delegates from the nine militia districts of Mecklenburg County met to discuss the political crises in the colonies. The news of the battle of Lexington had reached them and in the early hours of the 20th of May, they drafted a resolution declaring Mecklenburg County free and independent of Great Britain. Twenty of the twenty-seven signers were connected with the seven Presbyterian churches. Capt. James Jack rode to Philadelphia to present the Declaration to the North Carolina delegation to the Continental Congress. The message was suppressed. The document was treasonous and the delegation was not ready for treason.

Ellen Eanes is a quiltmaker and a lover of quilts of all ages. Her address is: 21 Musket Trail, Simsbury,CT 06070.

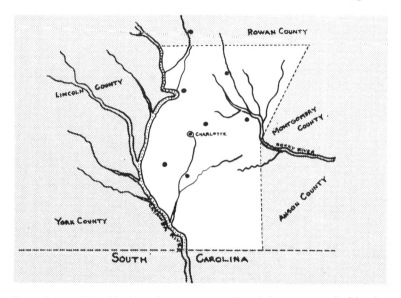

Fig. 1. Map of Mecklenburg County, 1789. Church locations marked by dots.

When John McKnitt Alexander's home burned in 1800, those original papers burned with it. Mr. Alexander, later that year, rewrote the Declaration from memory.[1] Other signers wrote affidavits testifying to the events of May 1775. In 1904, there was discovered in the archives of the Moravian Church a sketch of events of the period from 1775 to 1779. Translated into English it reveals:

> I cannot leave unmentioned at the end of the 1775th year, that already in the summer of this year, that is in May, June or July, the County of Mecklenburg in North Carolina declared itself free and independent of England, and made such arrangements for the administration of the laws among themselves, as *later* the Continental Congress made for all. This Congress, however, considered these proceedings premature.

During the Revolutionary War, Lord Cornwallis, after suffering a bitter defeat at the battle of King's Mountain, occupied Charlotte for two weeks. His foraging parties met such resistance that the area was labeled a "veritable hornet's nest of resistance." The descendants of these "hornets" still live in Mecklenburg County and can repeat the stories of that time and their families' part in history.

I became involved in this history because in January 1981, five Broderie Perse quilts owned by the Mint Museum of History in Charlotte were shown to me by the assistant curator, Barbara Taylor. A few weeks later, four more were brought to the museum on a "Quilt Identification Day." These four had been made by one woman who died in 1835. All nine quilts had a central medallion motif, but different designs. The chintz fabrics used for the centers and embellishment were identical in two quilts made by different women. The next year, two quilts with a Tree of Life design came to my attention. One was dated 1826. I was able to trace the genealogy of the makers of three of the museum's quilts and the others as well. When all my information was put together, I realized these quiltmakers had many common bonds and if not related by marriage, had connections through business or the church. The names show up in all the local histories: Davidson, Alexander, Lee, Orr, Wilson, Monteith, Harris. As Elizabeth Davidson, donor of two of the quilts to the museum, and my guide to much of my investigation, said: "If we aren't kin, we're connected."

These nine quilts from Mecklenburg County, if not kin, are definitely connected. They were made within a period of forty years at the very most, by women who knew each other well.

By all accounts, these people were educated, refined and wealthy; their hospitality was renowned. All lived on plantations, which were self-sustaining units. About the only items purchased were salt, sugar, coffee, tea, spices, snuff and fabrics such as calico and chintz. Cotton and wool were produced and woven on the plantations for family use, as well as clothing for the slaves.

Their parties were most fashionable. Quiltings were common. The ladies arrived in the afternoon and quilted until dark. Then the candles were lit and the fiddlers started. Margaret Wilson's father, Maj. Tommy Alexander, a Revolutionary veteran, was noted for his fiddle playing at the dances. Guests remained all night, sleeping on pallets or trundle beds stored beneath the massive poster beds. The quilts in my study are all huge, made to cover the beds and drop to the floor, hiding the trundle beds.

Cotton had been important when the 19th century was underway, but the production of gold became the sustaining force in Charlotte's economy until the Civil War. Sam McCombs had a gold mine near what is now uptown Charlotte, in 1825. Other mines were located on Harris and Springs properties. Finally, on March 3, 1835, Congress authorized the erection of a branch of the United States Mint in Charlotte. It was a time of prosperity for those fortunate enough to own land and business establishments.

1. THE SALLY ROXANA WILSON CALDWELL QUILT

When the Rev. Craighead's daughter, Rachel, married David Caldwell in 1766, an outstanding family was produced. There were eight sons and a daughter; three sons became ministers and one a physician. One son, David Caldwell, opened his "Log College" in Guilford County in 1767, a school known as one of the best in the history of North Carolina. David had been taught by the Rev. Craighead, and was also a graduate of Princeton. His students studied the classics and became eminent statemen, lawyers, judges, physicians and ministers. Some were Congressmen, and five became Governors of states.[2]

One of David's students was Joseph Wilson, father of Sally Roxana Wilson Caldwell. David and Rachel's grandson, D.T. Caldwell, would later practice medicine with Sally Roxana's husband, Pinkney C. Caldwell.

In the year of Sally Roxana's birth, 1810, her father was elected to the legislature. Soon after this he made his home in Charlotte. The next years must have been exciting ones for the Wilson family. In 1812 Joseph was elected "Solicitor to the Mountain Circuit." He fearlessly prosecuted the lawless mountain men.[3] According to legend, he wore a white hat on his rounds and was frequently ambushed.[4] Joseph Wilson died in 1829, two years before Sally Roxana married Pinkney C. Caldwell on December 15, 1831.

All the quiltmakers in my study were Presbyterians except for Sally Roxana. She and her husband were of Quaker parentage. Persons of all religious denominations in Charlotte worshiped at one church until 1832, when the Presbyterians bought the property. St. Peter's Episcopal Church was begun when the founding members, including Sally Roxana, met at the home of her brother-in-law, William Julius Alexander, on December 20, 1844.

Little more is known about Sally Roxana. She and Pinkney had three children who lived to maturity. Pinkney became known as the most distinguished physician in Mecklenburg County, practicing

Fig. 2. Sally Roxana Caldwell quilt, 1833. Mint Museum of History, #H62.10.

with D.T. Caldwell, grandson of the famous Rev. Craighead.

Sally Roxana Wilson Caldwell died March 12, 1863 and is buried beside Pinkney and their son, Dr. Joseph Caldwell, in the old settlers' cemetery behind the First Presbyterian Church. This quiet oasis is a block away from the skyscrapers of present-day Charlotte.

Sally Roxana's quilt[5] is a central medallion motif, with a center diamond and two wide borders. A piece of fabric like that used in the outer border has been cut into triangles and seamed to make the center diamond. The four large white triangles sewn to the center have bouquets of pink roses appliqued in the center of each, with tiny buttonhole stitches. The border surrounding this is chintz, with flowers printed in a square motif. This type of fabric usually was cut apart to make pillows,[6] but she has used it in strips. The colors are pinks, yellow, greens. The outer border is dark brown on the edge with madder red roses printed in a scallop design on white. The overall impression is that of three fabrics pieced together instead of one (Figure 2). The center diamond and the outer border are quilted in small squares with double lines about 1/8 inch apart. The first border has been quilted in parallel diagonal lines. On the back, written in ink with fine handwriting, typical of the time, is "Sally Roxana Caldwell, 1833."

In 1962, Dr. Annie Parks McCombs donated Sally Roxana's quilt to the Mint Museum. It had come down to her through Sally Roxana's daughter, Catherine Guion, who left it to her daughter, Ferebe (Effie) McCombs, Dr. McComb's mother. At the time of the donation an insurance value of fifty dollars was placed on it.

2. THE SARAH A. HARRIS QUILT

To the east of Charlotte, on the way to Raleigh, lies a community called Harrisburg, named for the Harris families who had vast land holdings in that area. This is now part of Carrabus County, but until 1792 was part of Mecklenburg County.

Sarah A. Harris was the granddaughter of Samuel Harris, who died in 1825. His will mentions his granddaughter Sarah A. Harris, and grandson Isaac Harris. The Sarah A. Harris whose quilt we are interested in was also the granddaughter of Adam Alexander, a signer of the Mecklenburg Declaration.[7] One of the problems in pinpointing genealogy in this case is the proliferation of similar names. These early families were large; first cousins frequently had the same names. Sarah and Isaac were Alexander family names. Sarah was the daughter of Mary Shelby Alexander and Dr. Cunningham Harris who died January 10, 1814. In Samuel Harris' will, [8] he requested that Sarah and Isaac be allowed to live at the mansion house if they chose, and also provided for their education and clothing. In addition, Sarah was to receive $250, a bureau, one bed and furniture, one-half of the dresser furniture to her forever, also a saddle and bridle.

Sarah's birthdate is given as 1806; she married Dr. James Gilmer on March 3, 1830. Dr. Gilmer had a large medical practice about six miles northeast of Charlotte. Sarah died in 1832, childless. Dr. Gilmer married two more times, and the quilt Sarah made has been kept in the family of his third wife, Lizzie Alexander. Sarah's aunt, Sarah Shelby Alexander, married Capt. John Springs in 1777 and thus Sarah was a first cousin to Mary Springs, of whom we shall hear later.

Dr. Gilmer's granddaughter, Burwell Parrish, has the quilt now. Mrs. Parrish is ninety-two and remembers the story of the brown stain on the quilt. It seems a young man was visiting her family home in her mother's time. He was sleeping in a room which had Sarah's quilt on the bed. During the night a bad storm came up and a window was broken. Rain and sleet poured in, so he put the quilt against the window, where it froze. Mrs. Parrish says, "Mama couldn't get it down for three weeks."

Sarah Harris' quilt is a Tree of Life design. The tree, with six branches, covers an area equal to the size of a double bed mattress. The tree has been cut of blue and rosy red plaid fabric. There are palm leaves at the top and at the end of some branches, with flowers and trailing vines carefully appliqued with buttonhole stitches. At the base is a strip of flowers appliqued, with a bluebird in the center. Under this, quilted and corded, is the legend, "Sarah A. Harris July 14, 1826." She was twenty that year. This tree is surrounded by a trailing vine border of appliqued flowers on white, with an outer border of flowered chintz. The background fabric is homespun linen and the thread is linen, with hardly a break in it. It is quilted in parallel diagonal lines about ¼ inch apart, all over. The colors of the chintz flowers are rosy red, with some blue and brown, plus green leaves.

Mrs. Parrish cherishes the quilt, as does her niece, Mary Lacy Bost. Mary Lacy's mother had the quilt at the family home for many years. It will be passed down in the family.

3. THE NANCY LEE QUILT

Another quilt, similar to Sarah's, was given to the Mint Museum of History last spring as the result of some publicity about these Mecklenburg quilts. This quilt was in the trousseau of Nancy (Mrs. David) Lee. It was donated by Mrs. Virginia Lee Bell Rhodes, Mrs. Lee's granddaughter. Nancy lived to the end of the 19th century.

Mrs. Rhodes has a picture of her. She couldn't give any details about her grandmother, except that she was very hardy and "never lifted a hand."[9]

Nancy Lee's quilt is also a Tree of Life design. It has three borders. The outer border and the first border are of a medium blue chintz with pink roses. The middle border is white with 18 bouquets of flowers evenly spaced and appliqued. The tree in the center has been cut freehand from the blue chintz used in the outer border. There are seven branches on the tree, with a profusion of flowers here, there and everywhere. The quilt is very worn, with the bindings gone and the edges ragged.

Mrs. Rhodes says the Lees were founding members of Sharon Presbyterian Church and may have donated some of the land where the church now stands. Sharon Church was organized for a group of landowners in that area who formerly worshipped at Providence or Steele Creek. The first minister was the Rev. Samuel Williamson, the uncle of Adeline Orr Parks, another of our quiltmakers. The Lees reportedly owned 3,700 acres between Carmel and Park Roads. This area is now a suburb of Charlotte, with Sharon Church still attended by the descendants of the original founders.

QUILTS 4, 5, 6 and 7, THE ANN ADELINE ORR PARKS QUILTS

The Dalton Collection of four quilts are attributed to Ann Adeline Orr Parks, daughter of Mary (Polly) Williamson and John Hanna Orr, who were married in 1801, a few years after John had built a brick plantation house at Mallard Creek. This house still stands and is on the Historical Properties List. Adeline was born in 1803.

A cross-stitch sampler made by Adeline provides the clues to her family ties.[10] It lists two brothers for Adeline: James H. (later known as Harvey) and Samuel. When Adeline was small, her mother died, and her father remarried. On the sampler, four children of that marriage are listed: Martha A., Moses M., Emily Hannah and Elizabeth A.

The *Catawba Journal* of Tuesday, February 6, 1827, states, "Married in this town by the Rev. John Williamson, Mr. D. Parks of this town to Adeline Orr, daughter of Mr. John H. Orr." David Parks was a merchant and a farmer, with land in North and South

Carolina and Tennessee. His store is mentioned in Dr. J.B. Alexander's book about Mecklenburg County and Charlotte, but there is no clue as to the nature of the enterprise.

Charlotte was starting to grow about this time. The gold rush was on. More stores were opened. The townspeople had been worshipping at a church for all denominations from 1815, when it had begun, until the First Presbyterian Church was dedicated in 1823. Church records show Adeline and David were members of the First Presbyterian Church in 1832. That year David was elected a First Elder.

Adeline's daughter, Mary Adeline, was born in February 1835 and in September, Adeline died. The quilts apparently were preserved for Adeline's descendants by David's second wife. In 1837, David married Ann C. Byers in Iredell County. Ann raised Mary Adeline as her own.

About the time Mary Adeline was growing up, a teacher from New York State arrived in Charlotte to start a school. There had been private schools in Charlotte earlier. The New York teacher, Susan Davis Nye Hutchinson, left several interesting diaries in which she wrote of her travels and her teaching days. She mentions tea in Charlotte with Mr. and Mrs. Parks.[11] When Mary Adeline was seventeen, she married Mrs. Hutchinson's son, Ebenezer Nye Hutchinson. During the next six years, Mary Adeline had three infants who died, and one who survived her, David Parks Hutchinson. Mary Adeline died in 1858 at the age of twenty-three, and once again Ann Parks took over. She lived to be ninety years old, dying in 1890. In her will, she left her estate to her stepgrandson, David Parks Hutchinson, whom she had raised from infancy and whom she held in tenderest affection.

The four quilts Adeline made before her early death are in mint condition, except for one which has sustained some water damage, causing the brown dye in one of the chintzes to run. Quilt 4 is that quilt. It is a square center medallion, with a large bouquet of flowers cut from chintz, enclosed in a flower ring in the middle. Surrounding this ring are 8 smaller bouquets and in the corners of the square, four triangular shaped bouquets. All are appliqued on a field of white. This square is bounded by a narrow floral stripe, another slightly wider floral chintz border is pieced to that. It is the brown in this piece that has run. The next to outer border is white with 8 palm tree tops evenly spaced, with pheasants atop the leaves, with small flowers interspersed at even intervals. The outer border is a wide light flowered chintz with a dark brown scalloped edge. The scallops are encased with a narrow linen tape. It is diagonally quilted with three narrow lines spaced with one an inch wide.

Quilt 5 has a center diamond format in the medallion style. This center has a panel of chintz appliqued, the same fruit basket found in the quilt attributed to Achsah Goodwin Wilkins, circa 1830 in Dena Katzenberg's book on Baltimore quilts.[12] This center diamond is framed with a rich red and brown chintz used in the same width in the first and third borders. In the four corner triangles surrounding the center diamond are appliqued bouquets also exactly like ones in Mrs. Wilkins' quilt. In the white border between the two chintz ones, Adeline has put four pheasants where the diamond points meet the first border. This quilt has fine clamshell quilting in the center diamond, "rope" quilting; i.e., five narrow lines followed by a space about ¾ inch wide, repeated. The outer borders have parallel diagonal quilting at ¼ inch intervals.

Quilt 6 is also a medallion with a diamond center format. Inside the diamond is a floral bouquet surrounded by a ring of flowers. This particular chintz has been documented as circa 1815 and possibly printed for use as a center in a quilt. A picture of it is in Florence M. Montgomery's book PRINTED TEXTILES.[13] From that picture, I can see how Adeline cut away the ring of flowers and pieced the corner arrangements, to enlarge the design. The diamond is edged with a floral stripe. The corner triangles have sprays of pink and blue flowers appliqued. This is enclosed by a floral border, then another floral applique on white border with a wide flowered chintz border at the edge. The quilt has clamshell stitching fanning out from the center to the triangles. Small squares are quilted on the borders.

Quilt 7 is the most beautiful, in my opinion. Adeline has used the same type center floral panel in this medallion quilt as in Quilt 6. But she has taken the circle of flowers that encloses the center bouquet and arranged the pieces with concave edges toward the center, and the triangular bouquets turned point inward, to create an entirely different appearance. This is again enclosed in a floral stripe to delineate the diamond. The corner triangles have a bouquet centered in each. A white border is pieced to this with eight groups of identical flowers placed evenly around the quilt. Finally there is a white background floral chintz border with a dark floral stripe at the edge. The diamond and triangles have been quilted in a small clam-shell design, and the outer borders quilted with the diagonal parallel lines. The quilting is superb on all these quilts. The colors, rose, pink, green, yellow, are still vibrant. Family members say they were used early in this century for company and special occasions. These quilts remain with their present owner, May Orr Dalton, the widow of Adeline Orr's great-great grandson.

8, 9. THE ROCINDA WILSON AND SOPHINA ALEXANDER QUILTS

The last two quilts were donated to the Mint Museum by Eliza-beth Davidson. One was known to Elizabeth as the Rocinda Wilson quilt and the other as the Jane Sophina Monteith quilt. It was the search for those women that led me to Elizabeth and the plantation world she has known and heard of all her life. This area of Mecklen-burg County centers around Hopewell Church. Much of the land today lies under Lake Norman, a lake made by the Duke Power Company when it dammed the Catawba River. But rolling hills and open fields and woods must look much the same as they did when Rocinda and Sophina were young. The roads then were dirt. Every woman rode horseback. The fields were planted in cotton.

Rocinda Winslow Wilson was born probably between 1775 and 1785. Her father, Moses Winslow, had a plantation near Centre Church, to the north of Hopewell. He had married Jean Osborne, the sister of Col. Adlai Osborne. When the soldiers of Lord Corn-wallis, heading towards Salisbury, reached Moses Winslow's home, they tried to burn it, knowing the owner to be a man of prominence and a member of the Provincial Congress. As the soldiers were offer-ing indignities to Mrs. Winslow, Lord Cornwallis himself rode up and order his men to desist and put out the fire.[14]

When Rocinda married William Jack Wilson around the turn of the 19th century, she entered one of the most distinguished families in Mecklenburg County. Her father-in-law was Sam Wilson, Sr., a tremendously wealthy man of aristocratic lineage, who owned large plantations. The Wilsons lived on lands close to Hopewell Church.

Hopewell not only is remembered for its religious history; it has the graves of the earliest patriots in its graveyard.

Rocinda Wilson and her husband lived as neighbors with Robert (called Robin) and Margaret Alexander Wilson, Elizabeth Davidson's great-grandparents. They were jointly famous for their hospitality and magnificent parties. A relative writing in the 1920s said that they would be known as "sports" in his day. The Wilson houses are gone, stripped by scavengers for the woodwork and old locks. Elizabeth Davidson's mother managed to save some of the molding from Robin's home and it is now in Elizabeth's living room at Rural Hill.

Rocinda and William had three sons and a daughter who lived to adulthood. A baby son, Moses Winslow Wilson, who was born in 1804 and died in 1805 is buried in Baker graveyard at Centre Church. This is the main clue we have to Rocinda's age. Her will was recorded in 1845. When it was written her sons, Robert, James and Lafayette and daughter Dovey were grown. Dovey Dougherty had a daughter who was Rocinda's namesake at the time.

Her quilts were important to Rocinda. She mentions them in her will, along with slaves, furniture, silver, linen and, of course, money and lands. Her son James was to receive three quilts, one fine, two common. To Lafayette she left two calico quilts, one fine, one common; to granddaughter Rocinda Dougherty, one calico quilt, one white Marseilles quilt.

The quilt Rocinda's great-grandniece, Elizabeth Davidson, gave to the museum is also a large medallion style with a center diamond (Figure 3), but it is quite different from the previously described quilts.[15] The center diamond has a fruit basket applique identical to Adeline Orr Parks' Quilt 5, and the diamond is outlined with a narrow floral chintz stripe. But the large triangles attached to this each contain nine brown and white pieced stars. These are unique. Each star has an octagon center, with a point pieced to each side of the octagon. This large square is framed with a pieced border of squares and triangles, all brown and white. A wide white border encloses the whole field, with sixteen bouquets of flowers evenly spaced. The fabric is very faded and worn, and the original colors are hard to determine.

Jane Sophina Monteith was the granddaughter of Richard Barry,

Fig. 3. Rocinda Winslow Wilson quilt, circa 1830–1840. Mint Museum of History, #77.102.

a signer of the Mecklenburg Declaration. Richard Barry was a neighbor of Moses Winslow at Centre Church. When the first Presbyterian services were held in that vicinity, they took place under a tree in his yard. According to tradition, the noted Dr. John Thomson preached "in the blacksmiths grove, now the grounds of the Presbyterian Church."

Sophina's mother, Violet, was Richard's daughter. Sophina was born in 1809 and married Andrew A. Alexander on March 24, 1840. They had two daughters and three sons. William Abner married

Rocinda Wilson's niece, Margaret Elizabeth Hampton. Sophina died in 1895 and is buried at Hopewell.

Sophina's quilt (Figure 4) is a medallion with a center square containing a basket of flowers appliqued, with a small bunch of flowers in each corner of the square.[16] This is enclosed in a chintz border followed by a white border with sixteen bouquets of flowers evenly spaced. A floral chintz border finishes it off. The applique work is done with tiny buttonhole stitches. This quilt has elaborate quilting in the white parts—stuffed grapes and leaves, with meandering background quilting. Sophina stitched her initials JSM in an oval of stuffed "grapes."

While Rocinda and Sophina were living in the Hopewell area, their neighbors were the Davidsons and the Brevards. Major John Davidson was a signer of the Mecklenburg Declaration. He had a thriving blacksmith business there, supplying the necessary iron tools for the plantations. He owned thousands of acres in the vicinity and built his home Rural Hill in 1787. Rural Hill is described in THE SQUIRES OF SPRINGFIELD by Katherine Wooten Springs.

It was an imposing two-story house of dark pressed brick, with massive Corinthian columns supporting the roof, which extended over wide piazzas, front and rear. On the main floor, the partitions between the spacious parlors could be raised from the floor and fastened to the ceiling with immense hooks, thereby throwing the rooms together for balls and important occasions.

The mansion was the scene for many parties. In a letter to Mary Springs, Elizabeth Davidson's great-grandmother, from Mary Warren in 1800, written at the Davidson plantation, Mary Warren says: "I am so engaged in frolicking, for there is nothing here among us but quiltings and weddings..." A month later she wrote: "I have just returned from another wedding. Young Mr. Davidson is married to Sally Brevard in Centre."[17]

The story of that courtship has survived for generations:

One morning after a hard rain, Major John Davidson called his son, Jacky, and said, "While the ground is too wet to plow, go and get your horse saddled and get yourself dressed. Go over to Adam Brevard's and court Sally. I think she will make you a good wife. Now you have no time to fool about it,

Fig. 4. Jane Sophina Montieth quilt, circa 1830–1840. Mint Museum of History, #77.67.

the ground will be dry enough to plow tomorrow."[18]

Jacky went like a dutiful son and Sally accepted his proposal. They had ten children. One son, Brevard, would marry Mary Laura, the daughter of Mary Springs, in 1832.

The Springs family saved their letters, and I am indebted to them for many of the descriptions of social life then. Mary Springs heard from her sister, Ginny Alexander, in 1803.

My Dear Mary,
I am still in the land of the living, thank the Lord. I have

been at (indecipherable) Ford since the first of September until last Monday. I came home. The people there is so hide bound between religion and the thoughts of high life, that you may know, I did not have much satisfaction. I was to four quiltings, but not any dancing at one of them. There is a Miss Smith living in the City that was educated at the boarding school. She played on the forty pianeau that was the greatest curiosity I ever saw. Are you done you quilts? I was just going to begin mine. If the weather holds good and warm, if wishing won't get you here, I would have you for the great meeting comes on next week, and then busy quilting.[19]

When Mary Laura Springs married Brevard Davidson, the wedding took place at Springfield, the Springs plantation just over the border in South Carolina. As was the custom in the early years of the century, weddings were gala home events. The wedding ceremony was by candlelight, performed by the Rev. John Williamson, the minister at Hopewell.

Jacky Davidson gave Rural Hill to Mary and Brevard, who eventually had sixteen children. John Springs also provided for them generously. He gave Mary Laura another plantation of 959 acres, household items of furniture, linens, silver, livestock, horses, a wagon and harnesses, twenty slaves and cash to furnish the plantation, about $14,000 altogether. Brevard prospered, and by the Civil War was the wealthiest man in the county. Rural Hill burned in 1886. All that remains today are the stone pillars from the front. Today, Elizabeth Davidson and her brother John Springs live in what was the original kitchen house, greatly expanded. Across the road, about a quarter mile away, is the Davidson private "burying ground." Major John and Violet Wilson Davidson are here, and most of their descendants. Mary Laura and Brevard's son, Baxter, restored it, and Elizabeth sees that it is well kept.

When Elizabeth Davidson graciously loaned me books and papers from her family, she helped me to link together these names from the past. We tramped through the old graveyards and she introduced me to the owners of Cedar Grove and Holly Bend. The history of Mecklenburg County took on a personal meaning for me. I like to think the quilts have served a far greater purpose than their original one. Sarah Harris didn't know, when she signed her quilt in

1826, that she would die, childless, just a few years later. But the quilt's existence caused someone to ask, "Who was Sarah A. Harris?"

The men of Mecklenburg County have torn down all the old landmarks except for a few. However, these quilts remain as testimonials to a time long ago, a different kind of life. It was easy and it was hard. There were slaves to take care of mundane household tasks, and money to buy what they wanted. But wealth couldn't protect them or their loved ones from sudden death. This thread of fear about sickness runs through all their letters.

Still there was time to enjoy family and friends and to express their artistic talents and sewing abilities in their quilts. Their quilts show that a common style, the medallion, was prevalent at that time, made by the leisure class who had the time to make them and the money to buy the expensive chintzes. The applique quilts were cherished in particular, as they survive after so many years when others which were sturdier were used until they disintegrated.

The connection with the Presbyterian churches is paramount in joining the lives of these women. Their husbands were doctors, merchants, farmers, but all staunch supporters of the Presbyterian Church with the exception of Sally Roxana and Pinkney Caldwell.

Mecklenburg County grew slowly until recent years, thereby preserving the nature of the society. Descendants of the early families live in the county, frequently in the old homes. They do not need to search for identity; they know exactly who they are. They live with the history of Mecklenburg. And every May 20, they gather to celebrate Mecklenburg Declaration Day and to remember the exciting years when our quiltmakers were helping lay the groundwork for what was to come.

Notes and References:

1. Dr. John Brevard Alexander, HISTORY OF MECKLENBURG COUNTY, Observer Printing House, Charlotte, NC, 1902.

2. Samuel A'Court Ashe, ed., BIOGRAPHICAL HISTORY OF NORTH CAROLINA FROM COLONIAL TIMES TO THE PRESENT, Vol., Charles L. Van Nappen, Greensboro, NC, 1905–1917, pp. 206–213.

3. Papers accompanying quilt, Mint Museum of History, Charlotte, NC.

4. William Henry Foote, SKETCHES OF NORTH CAROLINA, HISTORICAL AND BIOGRAPHICAL, Robert Carter, New York, 1846.

5. Sally R. Caldwell Quilt, Textile #H 62.10, Mint Museum of History, Charlotte, NC.

6. Florence M. Montgomery, PRINTED TEXTILES, Viking Press, Inc., New York, 1970, pp. 356, fig. 420.

7. Biographical information on Adam Alexander family supplied by Katherine Wooten Springs.

8. Wills — North Carolina Museum of History, Raleigh, NC.

9. Conversation with Mrs. Rhodes.

10. Owned by May Orr Dalton (Mrs. Parks Dalton).

11. Copy of Diary in North Carolina Room, Main Library, Charlotte, NC.

12. Dena S. Katzenberg, BALTIMORE ALBUM QUILTS, Baltimore Museum of Art, [1980], p. 63.

13. Montgomery, p. 356.

14. Old newspaper clippings, date unknown, from the Charlotte Observer, supplied by Elizabeth Davidson.

15. Rocinda Wilson Quilt — Textile #77.102, Mint Museum of History, Charlotte, NC.

16. Jane Sophina Monteith Quilt, Textile #77.67, Mint Museum of History, Charlotte, NC.

17. Katherine Wooten Springs, THE SQUIRES OF SPRINGFIELD, William Loftin, Charlotte, NC, 1965.

18. Dr. John Brevard Alexander, REMINISCENCES OF THE PAST SIXTY YEARS, Ray Printing Co., Charlotte, NC, 1908.

19. Springs Papers — Wilson Library, Chapel Hill, NC, Southern Historical Collection.

Red Cross Quilts for the Great War

Nancy J. Rowley

Motivated by a sense of patriotism and invited by the media to participate in an event known as the Great War, women were inspired to join and raise money for the American Red Cross in the years between 1916 and 1920.

Our country had entered the war and many of our boys were being shipped to France to protect their homeland and serve their country. Others were drafted and sent by train to camps on the east coast to await orders. Magazines and newspapers kept those at home informed while creating a subtle atmosphere of urgency about serving and doing one's share for the war effort.

LADIES HOME JOURNAL, HARPERS BAZAAR, WOMEN'S HOME COMPANION and COLLIERS magazines all carried regular feature articles plying the possibilities for women to help. No aspect of life was exempt from the urgings. After women sent their husbands to the draft they were invited to step into the industrial or business world (out of necessity in any case) or to go to school to prepare for a nursing career. Those over twenty-five (only after you were twenty-five could you get a passport to the war zone) could volunteer for canteen and aid stations in France. Or one belonged to the Red Cross at home and raised money to be spent in the war effort. Sentiment ran high for 'our boys over there' and, to quote a favorite passage of the day, everyone 'did their bit.'

By 1917 the American Red Cross already had a huge networking system in the United States and had just entered France, the seventh foreign commission in their organization. To give an idea of the magnitude of the Red Cross influence at the time, the Northwestern area (Washington, Oregon and Idaho) had 113 chapters with an average

Nancy J. Rowley has just completed her master's work in textile conservation at the University of Idaho. Her address is: Box 8333, Moscow, ID 83843.

membership of 7,396 per chapter. There were 532 nurses enrolled and 279,000 members in the Junior Red Cross in this area alone.[1]

The Red Cross offered many the opportunity to serve. Newspapers and magazines spread the news of the Red Cross work. They published ideas for fund raising projects. Advertisers used pictures and caricatures of Red Cross nurses in their campaigns. Probably the largest organizational effort and influence other than the military systems, the Red Cross, in one way or another, indoctrinated thousands into its ranks at the time.

Encouraged that there was 'great work' for them to do, women developed a powerful spirit of service. Told there was not room for 'the parasite, the sluggard, the inefficient or the ignorant'[2], they responded by giving unselfishly. They were motivated to minister and assist through articles and advertisements in magazines and the circulation of posters picturing pathetic children in war torn countries or a soldier fighting 'huns.' They were influenced by theatrical productions raising money for the Red Cross by doing a play called "The Tragedy of Flanders," the art world creating propaganda posters and battle scenes, news media sending pictures of the war front into the mail box, and post cards manufactured to raise money for orphans or French revitalization. Stimulated by a music world that was singing 'Anchors Aweigh' and 'Over There' and had George M. Cohan doing patriotic musical productions, women answered the call to 'do their bit.'

MODERN PRISCILLA, LADIES HOME JOURNAL, WOMEN'S HOME COMPANION and HARPERS BAZAAR are said to have ultimately started the twentiety century's first quilt revival by urging women to "Make Quilts—save the blankets for our boys over there."[3] However, this paper will be mainly concerned with those quilts made in response to efforts made to raise money for the Red Cross. These appear to be isolated efforts at quiltmaking.

The autograph quilt, a take-off on earlier friendship and album quilts, was designed to raise money by selling the privilege to 'sign' a block. These blocks then formed the quilt top which was usually auctioned or raffled. All of these monies then went to the Red Cross.

In a search to find autograph quilts made especially to raise money for the Red Cross, I found two in the American Red Cross

Museum in Washington, D.C. One was from Corvallis, Oregon with 42 red crosses appliqued on top and a blue border. It was presented to the Red Cross in 1922.[4] The other is an autograph quilt made in Santa Monica, California by seventh and eighth grade children. The series of red crosses have autographs over all and contain the written signatures of more than 100 contemporary people such as President and Mrs. Wilson, Colonel Theodore Roosevelt, Helen Keller, Sarah Bernhardt, John Philip Sousa and George Cohan.[5] There are also autograph quilts in the Albany Historical Society in Sabetha, Kansas and the Los Angeles County Museum collection.

Three Red Cross autograph quilts to be discussed here, are in the Latah County Historical Society collection in Moscow, Idaho. One quilt, maker unknown, reflects history of the Moscow area through embroidered names. Two of the quilts were made by Alma Lauder Keeling, who still resides in Moscow, and are referred to as the Oregon quilt and the French Orphan quilt.

The Moscow History quilt top (Figure 1) is covered with red crosses, machine appliqued onto a white ground. Ninety-five of these crosses in the center have embroidered names on them.[6] The quilt is beautifully hand quilted.[7] The donors of the quilt, Mr. and Mrs. Merrill Green, do not remember the quilt being made but believe it was done to raise money. It was part of the estate of Merrill Green's brother. The names are of people who had businesses or were in other occupations in the Moscow area during the Great War. Through interviews, old copies of local papers and the University of Idaho college annual I have identified a druggist, a realtor, several store owners and shopkeepers, clerks, a bank president and his cashier, meat packers and a butcher, laundry owners, a dressmaker, teachers, a postal clerk, a tailor, hotel owners, grain and poultry dealers and several farmers and housewives. Mrs. J.J. Day, whose name is embroidered in the center cross, was the wife of the owner of Day Mines in North Idaho, a mine still on the stock exchange.

The Oregon quilt is pieced of red and white crosses with blue borders surrounding them. Names of contributors are embroidered throughout and "Oregon 1918" is embroidered in the center cross. The quilt has a light batt and was quilted by Alma Lauder Keeling.[8]

Mrs Keeling made the quilt while living on her brother's home-

Fig. 1. Moscow History Red Cross quilt. Latah County (Idaho) Historical Society. Maker unknown.

stead near Arlington, Oregon. In ill health at that time, Alma describes herself

> "with much time on my hands.... We didn't even have a radio in those days, as they became popular later.... Of course, all the people of our country (USA) were busy *raising money for the Red Cross* (her emphasis). The idea occurred to me to make the

Fig. 2. Oregon Red Cross quilt (corner panel). Latah County Historical Society. Maker: Alma Lauder Keeling. Inscribed "Oregon 1918."

red cross quilt and have everyone I could contact donate 'so much' to have their names embroidered on the quilt. Most of those donations were only $1.00, but there were also those who gave more for a more conspicious place on the quilt.

I really don't know where I got all those names on the Red Cross quilt for our homestead cabin was miles from even a store. All the money was turned over to the Condon, Oregon, chapter of the Red Cross! I didn't even take out the cost of the goods in the quilt, as that, and the hours of work on it, were my donation to the war effort."[9]

Alma sat with the quilt over her knees to warm her from the autumn chill already in the air the day we visited about her quilts. She probably purchased the fabric from Sears, as she remembered her brother spent hours poring over their catalog. She designed the pattern herself. When I asked if she had made other quilts she answered an emphatic "No, that was work for grandmothers."

The story of the French Orphan quilt is told in Alma Lauder Keeling's own words.[10] She donated the quilt to the Historical Society in 1973 and it was accompanied by a letter explaining her work:

Fig. 3. French Orphan quilt. Latah County Historical Society. Maker: Alma Lauder Keeling. Inscribed "Orphelinat des Armees 1919."

"During the first World War there was a great deal of pressure on for people in the USA to 'adopt' (by long distance) the children orphaned by the War. I had a Sunday School class of Junior high girls in the Christian Church here at the time (Moscow), and we all wanted to help. The War was over, but the devastation was not, and many many children of French soldiers had been orphaned and made homeless by the holocaust.

While still in the trenches, the French soldiers who had a gift for drawing had made many designs depicting the tragedy of the War, and these were later made into postcards to be sold to help support the war orphans. My class purchased the cards and we sold them to interested persons.

Then the idea of raising money by the quilt came to us, and the girls were enthusiastic! The first year our own little class 'adopted' one orphan at $36.00, and when the quilt was finished in 1919 we had taken in enough money to adopt two!

When the Red Cross had its big auction sale of donated articles at Third and Main our quilt was donated to raise further money for the work of the Red Cross in the devastated area of the War.

My dad (Wylie A Lauder) who had watched with interest the making of the quilt, decided he would bid it in for me, no matter how high it went. So he was there and did just that! I believe the quilt sold for $32.00—just four dollars less than enough to support another war orphan. But this went to the Red Cross for the same work of rehabilitation, so my girls were happy. This was, of course, only the quilt top then, but mother had it lined and bound and took it to Los Angeles with us when we spent six months there. Few people had gone back to hand quilting then, so she had the work done by a shop there which specialized in machine quilting.

A word about the replicas of the trench drawing, which I enlarged.

No. 1 depicts two orphan children at their father's grave. (note his cap on the cross, and the mourners' arm bands on the children.)

No. 2 depicts a lost child in a bombed out town, crying for her family.

No. 3 depicts a mother and her children sitting among the debris of their home, not knowing where to go or what to do now.

No. 4 shows two orphans pulling the bell at the entrance of a war-orphanage, seeking admittance. Obviously both mother and father are gone and all they have left in the world is bound up in what they are carrying with them. Notice the tri-color flags over the door.

We could think of no better captions for the four pictures than Jesus' own words; "I was hungry and you gave me meat" "I was thirsty and you gave me drink" "I was naked and you

clothed me" "I was a stranger and you took me in". The lesson
was clear to the girls: "Inasmuch as you have done it unto the
least of these ... You have done it unto me."

It was a very satisfying and worthwhile project for all of us.

A word about the embroidery on the quilt. It was all done
in "outline stitch" with No. 50 Turkey red thread, except the
white stars on the American Flag — which were done with
single strand white embroidery floss.

The motto (Orphelinat des Armes) means in French,
Orphans of the Army.

The gold stars are, of course in memory of our own American soldiers killed in the war.

The money paid by friends and/or relatives of the dead was
as follows:

    (a) The two names in the center block netted $5.00
        each.

    (b) The gold stars on the four sides were $2.50 each.

    (c) All other names were $1.00 each.

The material for the quilt was all donated by the maker of
the quilt, or her generous dad who had watched with interest
the work being done — which took about three months."[11]

Alma's letter more than anything gives us a feel for what was hap-
pening at the home front. Although the autograph quilt may have
been made during a time when there was a push for making quilts to
economize or "do your part," those I have mentioned seem to be
single efforts rather than a movement. As Alma's letter indicates 'few
people had gone back to hand quilting then, so she had the work
done by a shop which specialized in machine quilting.' This occurred
well after the war was over. The autograph quilts were being made
by women (or children) answering a plea for help, often a newcomer
to quilting who saw her work as a task to aid in the war effort rather
than a revival of quiltmaking. The main impetus was the raising of
money in aid of the Red Cross programs.

Notes and References:

1. The American Red Cross Annual Report, year ended June 30, 1919.
2. My own accumulation of adjectives gleaned from selected copies of LADIES HOME JOURNAL, 1917, 1918, and 1919 and WOMEN'S HOME COMPANION, 1917, 1918 and 1919.
3. Cuesta Benberry, "The 20th Century's First Quilt Revival," QUILTER'S NEWSLETTER, October 1979, Issue 116.
4. Quilt, Red Cross, 60.21, American Red Cross Museum.
5. Quilt, Red Cross, 22.23, American Red Cross Museum.
6. Quilt, 76.05.1, Latah County Historical Society.
7. Interview with Mr. and Mrs. Merril Green, 9/13/1982. Interview with Mrs. Catherine Short, 9/29/1982.
8. Quilt, Latah County Historical Society.
9. Letter written to Nancy Rowley by Alma Lauder Keeling 9/22/1982. Interview with Alma Lauder Keeling 9/20/1982. With permission.
10. Quilt, 73.14.39, Latah County Historical Society.
11. Letter in quilt file, 73.14.39, Latah County Historical Society. Used with permission.

Bibliography

COLLIERS MAGAZINE, 1918, 1919.

HARPERS BAZAAR, 1918, 1919.

Fisher Ames, Jr. AMERICAN RED CROSS WORK AMONG THE FRENCH PEOPLE, The MacMillan Company 1921.

Foster Rhea Dulles, A HISTORY OF THE AMERICAN RED CROSS, Harper & Bros., New York, 1950.

GEM OF THE MOUNTAINS, University of Idaho Year book, 1917–18, 1918–19.

Barbara Jones and Bill Howell, POPULAR ARTS OF THE FIRST WORLD WAR, Blue Star House, Highgate Hill, London, 1972.

String Quilts

Pat Nickols

String quilts are constructed from a large number of scraps using the pressed-work technique.[1] They were made as utility quilts, because this technique is fast, simple and practical. One wonders if another name for this technique could be "the unworthy quilt" as we find many single blocks, unfinished tops and only a few string quilts. These quilts were utility bed covers, "using quilts," and were indeed used up. Possibly this is why there has been little research on this topic.

The term "string" is derived from the small, narrow scraps of fabric generally used to make these quilts. The strings were often strips of fabric left over from cutting out a garment.[2] The term "string" means a scrap that is longer than it is wide. Occasionally the scraps used were large chunks or irregular shapes. The scarcity of fabric was a constant concern for the early quiltmaker. In making a string quilt she did not trim her scraps to make pieces of consistent size of shape. She used her fabric as it was available. Her need was to complete the quilt and use it.

Although thrift and need were the primary reason for string quilts, they were not lacking in design and beauty.[3] In discussing examples of string quilts I will show that in spite of their humble origins many of the creations were carefully planned to produce artistic results, true graphic art.

String work is created on a foundation, either paper or fabric. Two strings are placed right sides together on the foundation and seamed straight across by hand or machine stitching through the foundation. Then the top fabric is folded back, covering the seam. It is finger pressed or ironed open to keep it in the new position. This process is repeated until the foundation is covered with strings. Jean

Pat Nickols is a quiltmaker and avid student of quilt making. Her address is: 7055 Country Club Drive, Anaheim, CA 92807.

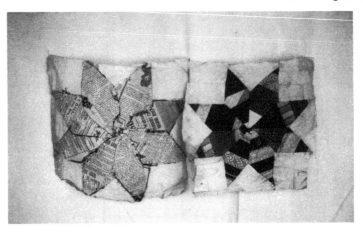

Fig. 1. String Star blocks on newspaper foundation from Vicksburg, Mississippi, 1903. Author's collection.

Dubois in her book THE WOOL QUILT gives clear directions and explanation for this technique.[4]

The art of taking small bits and pieces of used and unused material to create a fabric is well illustrated by a quilt made by Susan McCord from Indiana in 1845. Susan pieced thousands of irregularly shaped red and green scraps to make the leaf and petal shapes. Then she appliqued the string leaves on the solid green twisting vine. This 80" x 76" quilt is a magnificent example of balanced design and well coordinated color using the string technique.[5]

Geometric shapes, particularly diamonds and squares, were a favorite with the quiltmakers.[6] Diamonds usually used a random selection of colors and prints stitched across the width of the shape to the foundation. Diamonds were then pieced to obtain a star[7] (Figure 1). Usually the strings are stitched by hand as pick up work then the units are joined by machine. However examples of all hand, all machine or a combination can be seen. The block could then be completed by piecing in the background or by appliqueing the star to a whole cloth.[8] A seven pointed String Star top from mid-Missouri, circa 1930, is an illustration of the applique technique. In this case the foundation cloth is salt and sugar sacks as evidenced by the advertis-

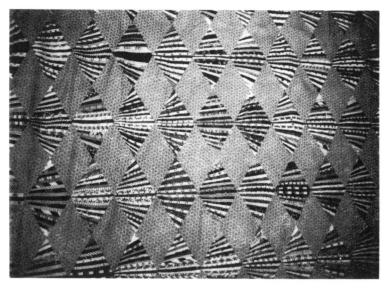

Fig. 2. *String Fan*, circa 1900. *Author's collection*.

ing markings still visible on the back. The border or joining strips of orange fabric are made of Purina Feed sacks.[9]

When squares were chosen, the strings usually were placed diagonally and a secondary pattern emerged.[10,11] In some cases these blocks were set on point, alternate block setting. Scrap selection (or lack of) did not mean loss of harmony. Repeated use of a blending fabric indicated the colorist was very aware of her pallet and knew how to use it. An example of this is shown by String Fan, circa 1900 (Figure 2). The diamond shape has been covered with red strings alternating with a random selection of scrap fabrics arranged in a fan design. The diamonds were then set in alternate blocks with a pink and white print fabric. The fans seem to dance across the quilt.[12]

Some contained crazy quilts are actually further examples of string quilts.[13] Perhaps a more accurate term for some contained crazy quilts would be "contained string quilts."[14] A string quilt is constructed by using a foundation, pressed work technique and straight seams. Often a contained crazy quilt or more accurately a contained string quilt is constructed by the string method, using the pressed technique and straight seams, rather than the usual crazy patchwork method.

Another type of string quilt is the suttles variation.[15] Suttles is a term used in Nova Scotia to refer to a bag of scraps or "the suttles bag."[16] Suttles is a pattern using a shape of three or more sides in the center of the block. Strings are sewn on this core to cover the desired shape. It could be compared to a free form log cabin block.[17]

When we examine a completed string quilt, the quilting is usually an all over pattern or utility quilting. The most common one is called by various names: shell, plate, fan or waves. A notable exception is a 1930s octagonal star quilt of multi-color string pieces and white, with a pink backing. The marking and quilting were done from the back with no reference to the front patterns. Double feathered circles with diamond grid centers and feathered lyre were quilted, truly a magnificent quilt.[18]

When our country was first developing and frontiers opened expanding westward, women met the need of their families by learning to adapt to a harsh and often isolated life. They were quick to utilize their scant, few possessions to the fullest. Recycling garments and all fabrics was a necessary part of their lives. The Scrap and string quilts they pieced brought not only warmth, but a practical and decorative solution to the bleakness of their lives... Those early quilts exemplify the intuitive and appreciation of beauty expressed by women untutored in the arts. Their skill at combining 50–200 different scrap-segments into one unifying, artistic design reveals them to be skilled craftswomen.[19]

Examples of string quilts have been found in New York, Michigan, Alabama, Mississippi, Tennessee, Texas, Illinois, Indiana, Missouri and Kansas. I feel there are opportunities for additional research on string quilts. Therefore I hope readers will look for further examples so more study can be done on this fascinating topic.

Notes and References:

1. Jean Dubois, THE WOOL QUILT, La Plata Press, Durango, CO, 1978, p. 129.
2. Bonnie Leman, QUICK AND EASY QUILTING, Moon Over the Mountain, Wheatridge, CO, 1972, p. 53.
3. Margaret Cavigga, QUILTS, Shufunotomo Ltd., Japan, 1981, pp. 71-72.
4. Dubois, pp. 132-139.
5. Robert Bishop, NEW DISCOVERIES IN AMERICAN QUILTS, Dutton, New York, 1975, pp. 112-113.
6. Jonathan Holstein, THE PIECED QUILT, New York Graphic Society, Boston, 1973, plate 30.
7. Ruth McKendry, TRADITIONAL QUILTS AND BED COVERINGS, Van Nostrand Reinhold, Toronto, 1979, fig. 176 (p. 104).
8. Thos. K. Woodard and Blanche Greenstein, CRIB QUILTS AND OTHER SMALL WONDERS, Dutton, New York, 1981, p. 33.
9. Quilt in author's collection.
10. Leman, p. 59.
11. Holstein, plate 81.
12. Quilt in author's collection.
13. Woodard, p. 33, plate 37.
14. Cyril I. Nelson, QUILT ENGAGEMENT CALENDAR 1981, Dutton, New York, 1980, p. 39.
15. Lenice Ingram Bacon, AMERICAN PATCHWORK QUILTS, Bonanza Books, New York, 1980, p. 145.
16. Marjorie Puckett, STRING QUILTS 'N THINGS, Orange Patchwork Publishers, Orange, CA, 1979, p. 39.
17. Nelson, p. 55.
18. Quilt in collection of Marjorie Puckett.
19. Puckett, preface.

The Hall/Szabronski Collection at The University of Kansas

Barbara Brackman

The Helen Foresman Spencer Museum of Art at the University of Kansas in Lawrence, Kansas has an impressive collection of over 200 quilts, and an equally impressive collection of quilt research materials. The quilts are there primarily due to the collecting of Sallie Casey Thayer; the other quilt-related materials are due to the collecting of two women—Carrie Hall and Elizabeth Szabronski.

Like many other museums the University of Kansas's art museum is based on the collection of a private individual. In 1917 the University received a gift of over 5000 items from Sallie Casey Thayer, a wealthy Kansas City woman who was an early collector of American antiques and other art.[1] Mrs. Thayer collected eclectically. Her interests included Japanese prints, European glass and American quilts. The nucleus of her collection became the basis of the art collection at the University of Kansas which was first housed in the Spooner-Thayer Museum, dedicated in 1928. In the textile collection were Mrs. Thayer's 53 quilts, including a One Patch[2] supposedly from the family of Alexander Hamilton[3] (Figure 1) and a Medallion with eight-pointed stars.[4] The chintz medallion in that quilt is attributed to John Hewson[5] (Figure 2).

The new museum's first curator was Minnie Moodie, who advanced to that position after serving as secretary to the University chancellor for 22 years.[6] She spent years working with Mrs. Thayer and her collection while it was in storage at the University waiting for a permanent home. During this time the collection was soaked in a Kansas thunderstorm which broke out the windows in the storage area. Then the collection was loaned to a museum in San Diego where Mrs. Thayer threatened to leave it if the University did not

Barbara Brackman is a quilt teacher, lecturer and compiler of pieced quilt patterns. Her address is: 500 Louisiana, Lawrence, KS 66044.

Fig. 1. One Patch quilt with fringe, c. 1800. Maker unknown. Cat. #28.914, Helen Foresman Spencer Museum of Art, University of Kansas. Photo courtesy Spencer Museum.

establish the promised art museum. When plans were made to con-vert the Spooner Library to a museum Miss Moodie's acquired ex-pertise with the Thayer collection was a prime qualification for the position of curator.

After the opening of the Spooner-Thayer Museum of Art in 1928 one of the visitors who came to view the quilts was Carrie Hall of nearby Leavenworth, who had been a seamstress for over forty years.[7] Madam Hall (as she called herself professionally) had become interested in quilts after World War I, looking for some hand work to occupy time that had been spent knitting for the Red Cross.[8]

Madam Hall was an incorrigible collector and her new hobby

Fig. 2. Medallion with Eight Point Star, 1848. Signed Elizabeth Hart. Cat. #28.916. Helen Foresman Spencer Museum of Art, University of Kansas. Photo courtesy Spencer Museum.

quickly developed into a large collection of quilt patterns and clippings from periodicals. She says in her book THE ROMANCE OF THE PATCHWORK QUILT IN AMERICA that she decided to make a block of every pattern[9] but, like many of the rest of us quilters who might aspire to a similar goal, she had no idea of the quantity of patterns there were. During the 20s and 30s she had many patterns to choose from. Farm magazines, women's magazines, periodicals of general interest and, of course, needlework magazines all printed quilt patterns. Madam Hall's collection of these patterns illustrates the vast number of such designs available to the quilter in the central Midwest at that time.

As Hall neared retirement age her dressmaking business declined. Always resourceful, she turned her quilt block collection into a career. She became a quilt lecturer, touring eastern Kansas and the vicinity with her "Quilt Talks." In a letter of 1938 she mentioned that she gave her talk over 80 times to various women's groups.[10] In her scrapbooks are clippings which describe the colonial costume she wore for the occasion and the collection of 500, then 600, then 1000 quilt blocks which she brought with her.[1]

The scrapbooks are a record of the "Quilt Talks"; they also record the quilt craze of the time. As a child Madam Hall had hoped to own a library when she grew up.[12] She achieved this goal, developing collections of books and clippings on numerous topics besides quilts. She collected books on Abraham Lincoln, Theodore Roosevelt, costume and travel.[13] In the early 30s she began collecting materials on quilts, the information going into her quilt scrapbooks and photographs of her quilt blocks into a book. With Rose Kretsinger of Emporia, Kansas, she wrote THE ROMANCE OF THE PATCHWORK QUILT IN AMERICA. The book is a potpourri of information, reading somewhat like a scrapbook itself, with photographs of antique and contemporary quilts of Kansas, some biographical notes, Mrs. Kretsinger's history of the art of quilting and, in the core of the book, an index to quilt patterns featuring photographs of her blocks.

In writing this book she visited The Spooner-Thayer Museum in Lawrence where she studied the quilts in the William Thayer Memorial Collection. Photographs of ten quilts from the collection are included in ROMANCE. While working with Miss Moodie on the project, Hall decided to donate to the Museum her collection of 1000 "quilt patches," as she calls them in the foreword to the book written in May, 1933.[14]

Over the next few years she sent parts of her collection to Lawrence and says in a letter dated 1938 that she is sending the last installment of blocks over in the suitcase which she used when she took the blocks with her on her speaking trips.[15]

In addition to the blocks she donated one of her quilts, The George Washington Bi-Centennial,[16] and the scrapbooks, patterns, pamphlets and books she had collected. The books were placed in the University's Watson Library where they were in general circulation until the late 1970s. They are now in the closed stack collection of the Art Library at the Spencer Museum.

The quilt blocks and the archival material were stored with the textile collection at the Spooner-Thayer Museum. In 1978 the University transferred its art collection to the new Helen Foresman Spencer Museum of Art on the campus. The Spooner Building now houses a museum of anthropology.

When Madam Hall donated the blocks she wrote to Miss Moodie:

"You will not only have the finest collections of patterns, etc., pertaining to patchwork in the U.S. but also in the world —for I feel safe in saying there is no other like it."[17]

The quilt block collection at the Spencer Museum now numbers 1057. Hall's book contained photos of 854. Volunteers working with the blocks have discovered that nine are missing (see Appendix 1). Over the early years the Museum lent the blocks several times, loaning them to magazines to be photographed or to be displayed at the State Fair in Hutchinson. The recent move to Spencer Museum, plus increased funding for museum staff and an increased awareness of the blocks' value will possibly assure that none will be lost in the future.

In 1974, when Elizabeth Szabronski retired with her husband to Gulfport, Florida, she donated her library of quilt books, patterns and research materials to the Spooner-Thayer Museum. She wrote to Jean Mitchell, a museum volunteer working with the Szabronski materials, "I knew Carrie Hall's blocks were there and somehow I felt they should be together."[18]

Mrs. Szabronski had lived in Levittown, New York where she, following in the tradition of Sallie Casey Thayer and Carrie Hall, was a collector. As Madam Hall's collection is a cross section of quilting in the twenties and early thirties, Mrs. Szabronski's collection is a cross section of the fifties and sixties.

There is a feeling among today's quilters that interest in quilting died out from World War II through the sixties, but the Szabronski collection of patterns and correspondence is evidence that there was a strong network of quilt historians, pattern collectors and quilters operating in the fifties and sixties. Mrs. Szabronski subscribed to a number of quilt pattern publications including LITTLE 'N BIG[19]

AUNT KATE'S QUILTING BEE[20] and HOBBIES, CRAFTS AND QUILT NEWS.[21] These magazines reprinted out-of-print patterns from the periodicals of earlier days; they held contests for new patterns and they fostered communication between collectors, primarily with Round Robins which were pattern trading networks. The magazines were short-lived, often mimeographed and certainly primitive by the standards of the eighties, but they are useful in documenting mid-twentieth century quiltmaking and patterns.

In addition to quilt magazines, Mrs. Szabronski collected patterns from other sources of the day including the Stearns and Foster Company, the Needlecraft Company with the Old Chelsea Station address, and women's magazines. Like Hall she developed an index to the many patterns in her collection, but hers has never been published. She sketched a drawing of every pattern she found in the books, pamphlets and correspondence and filed them alphabetically on index cards, cross-referenced to other names for the same pattern with her source indicated. She donated these five boxes of index cards with approximately 5000 individual cards to the University of Kansas with her other quilt-related material.

During the 1970s several quilters have discovered the Hall/Szabronski collection of materials. They have provided inspiration and raw material for QUILT KANSAS! by Jean Mitchell[22] and my own AN ENCYCLOPEDIA OF PIECED QUILT PATTERNS.[23] Blocks and selections from the archival material have been exhibited twice. All the blocks were exhibited during the Kansas Quilt Symposium in 1978 and approximately 100 were shown at the Museum in the summer of 1981.

The archival material is now being organized by volunteers and it will soon be placed in the Art Library at the Spencer Museum of Art where it will be available to researchers in the closed stacks.

The quilt blocks will remain in the textile collection of the Museum. Jean Mitchell donated the profits from QUILT KANSAS! to provide for quilt conservation and storage. The Museum has purchased acid-free tubes to better store their quilts. The curator hopes to insert the quilt blocks in mylar envelopes and keep them contained in looseleaf notebooks where they could be accessible for examining both sides of the block without actually touching the fabric. Each block would be placed in a three-sided, inert mylar envelope which would allow for air circulation and occasional removal for other display.

Through the foresight of Thayer, Hall and Szabronski the University of Kansas has, not only a fabulous collection of quilts, but one of the very few public collections of archival materials related to the art. It is hoped that in the future more such collections will be donated to museums, libraries and specialized study centers. Perhaps the American Quilt Study Group will develop a research center. A repository for materials such as patterns, blocks, letters, published material and other archival information on quilts may inspire today's quilters to emulate Carrie Hall and Elizabeth Szabronski in their collecting, their organizing and, finally, their generosity in sharing their collections with future students of quilt history.

Appendix 1

BLOCKS MISSING FROM HALL COLLECTION

Name of Pattern	Location in Book*
Crazy	Plate I #2
St. Louis Star	Plate V #6
Kaleidoscope	Plate XI #7
Ornate Star	Plate XIII #1
Octagon Tile	Plate XVI #24
Double Peony & Wild Rose	Plate XXVIII #2
Water Lily	Plate XXXIII #4
Hickory Leaf	Plate XXXIII #14
Roman Stripe	Not pictured in ROMANCE but pictured on the cover of CRAFT HORIZONS, June 1966.[24]

*Carrie A. Hall and Rose G. Kretsinger, THE ROMANCE OF THE PATCHWORK QUILT IN AMERICA, (Caldwell, Idaho, 1935)

Appendix 2

BOOKS, PAMPHLETS AND PATTERNS IN HALL/
SZABRONSKI COLLECTION. Each item is marked as being
donated by Carrie Hall (CH) or Elizabeth Szabronski (ES).

A. BOOKS (ES)

Lilian Baker Carlisle, PIECED WORK AND APPLIQUE QUILTS AT
SHELBURNE MUSEUM, Shelburne, Vermont, 1957

Mildred Davison, AMERICAN QUILTS FROM THE ART INST-
TUTE OF CHICAGO, Chicago, 1966

Lydia Roberts Dunham, DENVER ART MUSEUM QUILT COLLEC-
TION, Denver, 1963

Ruth Finley OLD PATCHWORK QUILTS AND THE WOMEN WHO
MADE THEM, New York, 1929

Mavis Fitzrandolph and Florence M. Fletcher, QUILTING: TRADI-
TIONAL METHODS AND DESIGN, Leicester, England, 1955

Marie Knorr Graeff, HOME CRAFT COURSE, VOLUME 14, PENN-
SYLVANIA GERMAN QUILTS, Kutztown, PA, 1946

Carrie A. Hall and Rose G. Kretsinger, THE ROMANCE OF THE
PATCHWORK QUILT IN AMERICA, Caldwell, ID, 1936

Thelma Heath, HOW TO MAKE A REALLY DIFFERENT QUILT,
Bloomington, IL, n.d. Photocopy

Dolores A. Hinson, QUILTING MANUAL, New York, 1966

Stella M. Jones, HAWAIIAN QUILTS, Honolulu, 1930

Florence Peto, HISTORIC QUILTS, New York, 1939

Florence Peto, AMERICAN QUILTS AND COVERLETS, New York,
1949

Elizabeth Wells Robertson, AMERICAN QUILTS, New York, 1949

Sears, Roebuck and Co., SEARS CENTURY OF PROGRES IN
QUILTMAKING, Chicago, 1934

Victoria and Albert Museum, NOTES ON QUILTING, London,
1949

Victoria and Albert Museum, NOTES ON APPLIED WORK AND
PATCHWORK, London, 1959

Marie D. Webster, QUILTS: THEIR STORY AND HOW TO MAKE
THEM, New York, 1915

B. PERIODICALS AND PAMPHLETS IN SERIES INCLUDING PATTERNS AND CLIPPINGS

Aunt Kate (ES)
Glenna Boyd, AUNT KATE'S QUILTING BEE, Vinita, Oklahoma (periodical) Holdings: Vol. I, No. 1 (July, 1962) through Vol. V, No. 6, (December, 1966)
Glenna Boyd, AUNT KATE'S FOLIO OF ORIGINAL QUILTING DESIGNS, Vol. I, Vinita, Oklahoma, 1963
Glenna Boyd, AUNT KATE'S QUILTING BEE, BIG ANNUAL, NUMBER I, Burleson, Texas, 1970

Aunt Martha (Colonial Pattern Co.) (ES)
PRIZE WINNING DESIGNS (fragments) n.d., ca. 1931
THE QUILT FAIR COMES TO YOU (photocopy) n.d. ca. 1934
QUILT DESIGNS: OLD FAVORITES AND NEW #3175
AUNT MARTHA'S FAVORITE QUILTS #3230
QUILTS: MODERN-COLONIAL #3333
EASY QUILTS #3500
QUILT LOVER'S DELIGHT #3540
QUILTS: 14 QUILT PATTERNS PLUS BORDERS AND QUILTING DESIGNS #3614

Better Homes & Gardens (ES)
ADVENTURES IN NEEDLECRAFT, Des Moines, Iowa, n.d.
LAZY STAR (pattern), 1960

Capper's Weekly/Famous Features Syndicate
Margaret Whittemore, QUILTING: A NEW-OLD ART. Capper Publications, Topeka, Kansas, n.d. ca. 1930 (CH)
FLOWER QUILTS: A DOZEN FAVORITES FROM GRAND-MOTHER'S GARDEN #Q101, n.d. (ES)

Coats & Clark Company
GRANDMOTHER'S PATCHWORK QUILT DESIGNS, Book #20, WLM Clark Co., 1931, 2 copies (CH & ES)
GRANDMOTHER'S OLD FASHIONED QUILT DESIGNS, Book #21, WLM Clark Co., St. Louis, 1931, 2 copies (CH & ES)
GRANDMOTHER CLARK'S AUTHENTIC EARLY AMERICAN PATCHWORK QUILTS, Book #23, WLM Clark Co., St. Louis, 1932 (ES)

Betty Flack (ES)
Betty Flack & Claudine Moffat, ALLEMANDE LEFT, (Nancy Page
    reprints), ABC Publications, Shumway, IL and Valley Park, MO
BETTY'S APPLIQUE QUILTS, Book 1A, Shumway, IL
A CHILD'S ALPHABET
COVERLID CUTIES (Nancy Cabot reprints)
TEN APPLIQUE DESIGNS AS SHOWN IN REVIVAL OF OLD TIME
    PATCHWORK, ABC Publications, Shumway, IL (see Comfort)
Betty Flack (ed) LITTLE N BIG (periodical) Shumway, IL
    Holdings: Vol. 1 #5 (June 1964) through Vol. 2, #8 (Sept. 1965) plus
    Vol. 3 #1 & 2 (Feb. and March, 1966)
Betty Flack (ed), LITTLE N BIG ANNUAL, 1964
Betty Flack and Lucy Heddings, PATCHWORK, PATCHWORK,
    PATCHWORK, PATCHWORK, PATCHWORK, September 1963
Betty Flack & Claudine Moffat, PROMENADE (Nancy Page reprints)
Betty Flack, NANCY PAGE ON HOMEMAKING, ABC Publications,
    Shumway, IL and Valley Park, MO

4J's Bulletin (ES)
Joy Craddock, 4J'S BULLETIN, Denison, TX, #9, Sept, 1965

Good Housekeeping
GOOD HOUSEKEEPING'S QUILT BOOK, GHN 596 (ES)
Good Housekeeping Needlework and Sewing Center, QUILT MAK-
    ING AND QUILT PATTERNS, Hearst Publishing Co., New York,
    1963

Kansas City Star (CH)
Approximately 200 clippings from the Kansas City Star

Mary King (ES)
MARY KING'S PATTERN KEY, Embroidery House, Chicago, 1931
    (photocopy)

Arlene Klindt (ES)
Arlene Klindt (ed) HOBBIES, CRAFTS AND QUILT NEWS, Mary-
    ville, MO (periodical). Holdings: Vol. 1, #6 (August, 1962) through
    Vol. 1, #14 (April, 1963) plus Vol. 2, #3 (May, 1963) through
    Vol. 2, #7 (September, 1963)

Chatelaine (ES)
Ruth Zavitz and Wanda Nelles, "Make an Heirloom Quilt," CHATE-LAINE, Jan., 1964, Toronto, plus patterns ordered

Comfort (ES)
Mrs. Wheeler Wilkinson (ed) REVIVAL OF OLD-TIME PATCH-WORK AND APPLIQUE, A Photocopy published by ABC Publications, Shumway, IL, n.d. ca 1920 (copy ca. 1965)

Mrs. Danner (ES)
Scioto Imhoff Danner, MRS. DANNER'S QUILTS, ElDorado, KS, 1934
Scioto Imhoff Danner, MRS. DANNER'S SECOND QUILT BOOK, ElDorado, KS, 1934
Scioto Imhoff Danner, MRS. DANNER'S THIRD QUILT BOOK, El-Dorado, KS, 1954
Scioto Imhoff Danner, MRS. DANNER'S FOURTH QUILT BOOK, ElDorado, KS, 1958
Scioto Imhoff Danner and Helen Erickson, MRS. DANNER'S FIFTH QUILT BOOK, ElDorado, KS, 1970

Grandma Dexter (ES)
Fragments (pp. 3–24) of Grandma Dexter's Book 36B

Robert Frank Needlework Supply Company (ES)
E-Z PATTERNS FOR PATCHWORK AND APPLIQUE QUILTS, Robt. Frank Needlework Supply Co., Kalamazoo (photocopy)

Farm and Fireside (CH)
Clementine Paddleford, PATCHWORK QUILTS: A COLLECTION OF FORTY-ONE OLD TIME BLOCKS, Farm and Fireside, n.d.

Farm Journal (ES)
FARM JOURNAL AND FARMER'S WIFE QUILT PATTERNS, Farm Journal, Philadelphia, n.d.
FARM JOURNAL QUILT PATTERNS: OLD AND NEW, Farm Journal, Philadelphia, n.d.

Ladies' Art Company (ES)
QUILT PATTERNS, PATCHWORK AND APPLIQUE, Ladies' Art Co., St. Louis, 1928

QUILT PATTERNS, PATCHWORK AND APPLIQUE, Ladies' Art
Co., St. Louis (reprint)

700 OLDE TIME NEEDLECRAFT DESIGNS AND PATTERNS, House
of White Birches, Seabrook, NH (reprint of 1928 catalog included)

Lockport Batting Company (ES)
LOCKPORT PATTERN QUILTING BOOK, Lockport Batting, Lockport, NY, 1939

Martha Madison (Nancy Cabot Syndicate) (ES)
THE LITTLE CATALOG OF JUST QUILTS, Martha Madison
Needlework, NY

Ruby S. McKim (ES)
Ruby Short McKim, ADVENTURES IN NEEDLECRAFT, McKim
Studios, Independence, MO
Ruby Short McKim, DESIGNS WORTH DOING, McKim Studios,
Independence, MO

Claudine Moffat (ES)
Claudine Moffat, CLASSIC CONTEMPORARY OR COLONIAL
QUILTS & KIVVERS, Book 6, ABC Publications, Valley Park, MO
COUNTRY COUSINS (Nancy Cabot redrawn)
COZY COTTAGE COVERS, (Nancy Cabot redrawn)
DO SA DO KIVVERS, Pattern Book 53NP, 1964
JB'S HOBBY PATTERN MAGAZINE, (periodical) Valley Park, MO,
Holdings: Vol. 1, #11 (Nov., 1962) through Vol. 2, #12 (Dec., 1963)
JB NEEDLEWORK MAGAZINE, (periodical) Valley Park, MO,
Holdings: Vol. 3, #1 (Jan., 1964) through Vol. 4, #3 (Mar., 1965)
QUILTS AND KIVVERS #1 (Kansas City STAR redrawn)
QUILTS AND KIVVERS #2 (Kansas City STAR redrawn)
SCRAP BAG KIVVERS (Kansas City STAR redrawn)
THRIFTY WIFE KIVVERS (Kansas City STAR redrawn)
TWENTY-FIVE HEIRLOOM QUILTS—APPLIQUE (Kansas City
STAR redrawn)
Claudine Moffat and Betty Flack, PIGGY BANK KIVVERS, 1964
Claudine Moffat and Betty Flack, HOE DOWN KIVVERS, Book #52,
(Nancy Page redrawn)

Old Chelsea Station Needlecraft Company
AMERICAN HERITAGE QUILT BOOK (ES)
MUSEUM QUILTS, QUILT BOOK 2, Graphic Enterprises, Inc.
NEEDLECRAFT PATTERNS
NEEDLECRAFT PATTERNS
Plus fragments of other catalogs (ES)
Plus clippings pasted in a scrapbook (CH)

Anne Orr
Anne Orr, PATTERN BOOK, ANNE ORR QUILTS, Book 50, Nashville, TN, 1944 (ES)
THE LINCOLN QUILT PATTERN (CH)
THE ROOSEVELT QUILT PATTERN (CH) See Goodhousekeeping Magazine.

Prudence Penny (CH)
Prudence Penny, OLD TIME QUILTS: A COLLECTION OF OLD-TIME QUILT PATTERNS, Seattle POST-INTELLIGENCER, ca. 1927

Profitable Hobbies (ES)
Margaret I. Smith, "Selling Quilt Patterns by Mail," PROFITABLE HOBBIES, Jan., 1957. An article on Scioto Imhoff Danner.

Quilter's Newsletter Magazine (ES)
Bonnie Leman (ed.), QUILTER'S NEWSLETTER, Denver.
  Holdings: Vol. 1, #2, December, 1969 only

Rock River Cotton Company (ES)
Rock River Cotton Co., Janesville, WI, PATTERNS (9)

Carlie Sexton
Carlie Sexton, OLD FASHIONED QUILTS, Wheaton, IL, 1928, two copies (CH) (ES)
Carlie Sexton, YESTERDAY'S QUILTS IN HOMES OF TODAY, Successful Farming, Des Moines, IA, 2 copies (CH) (ES)
Barbara Bannister, FIFTEEN QUILT PATTERNS FROM OLD FASHIONED QUILTS BY CARLIE SEXTON, Bel Air Needlecrafts, Vanderbilt, MI, 1964 (Sexton redrawn) (ES)

Spool Cotton Company (ES)
QUILTS #1145,The Spool Cotton Co., 1945

Stearns and Foster Company (ES)
DIRECTIONS FOR QUILT MAKING BY HOME SEWING MACHINE,
   Stearns and Foster Co., Cincinatti, 1958, 2 copies
MOUNTAIN MIST BLUE BOOK OF FAMOUS QUILT DESIGNS,
   Stearns and Foster Co., Cincinnati, 1935
1957 MOUNTAIN MIST BLUE BOOK OF QUILTS, Stearns and Foster
   Co., Cincinnati, 1957
QUILT PATTERNS, OLD AND NEW, Catalog #33, Stearns and
   Foster Co., Cincinnati
QUILT PATTERNS, OLD AND NEW, Catalog #37, Stearns and
   Foster Co., Cincinnati, 1962
MOUNTAIN MIST BATTING wrappers with patterns numbered H,
   T, 21, 25B, 49, 54, 68, 73, 75, 87, 96, 98, 99, 102, 104, 108, 109, 113,
   116, 117, 126, 127

Taylor Bedding Mfg. Company (ES)
THIRTY-ONE QUILT DESIGNS, Taylor Bedding Mfg. Co., Taylor,
   TX

Walker Pattern Company (CH)
Mary Evangeline Walker and Lydia LeBaron Walker, GEORGE
   WASHINGTON BICENTENNIAL QUILT PATTERN

Marie Webster (CH)
Catalog of Marie Webster's patterns plus 2 patterns: SUNBONNET
   LASSIES AND SUNFLOWER QUILT

Marietta Welsh
Marietta Welsh, PATTERN CLUB, (periodical), Keyser, WV, Aug.-
   Oct. 1962, Books 2, 3 and 4 plus K.C. Star patterns (redrawn)

Women's Day (ES)
"Collector's Craft Book, Patchwork Squares," WOMEN'S DAY, June,
   1957
Rose Wilder Lane, "The Story of American Needlework #2: Patchwork," WOMEN'S DAY, April, 1961, plus patterns ordered
Rose Wilder Lane, "The Story of American Needlework #6: Applique," WOMEN'S DAY, November, 1961, plus patterns ordered

Women's World (ES)
THE PATCHWORK BOOK, The Manning Publishing Co., Chicago

C. MISCELLANEOUS MATERIAL

In Carrie Hall's Collection
6 scrapbooks containing patterns clipped from periodicals and articles on quilts and Carrie Hall
23 envelopes containing hand-drawn patterns from which blocks were made plus clippings from other patterns never made up. These have recently been filed in separate envelopes for each pattern by Betty Hagerman and Helen Ericson
48 hand-colored block illustrations
folder of unlabeled photographs of quilts not used in book
partial manuscript of book
1057 quilt blocks made by Carrie Hall
1 quilt: George Washington Bi-Centennial by Carrie Hall

Elizabeth Szabronski's Collection
5 index card file boxes with an index to quilt pattern sources filed alphabetically by name
12 folders containing tracings, clippings and mimeographed patterns filed alphabetically by name

Notes and References:

1. Carol Shankel, SALLIE CASEY THAYER AND HER COLLECTION, Lawrence, KS, 1976, p. 52
2. Pieced quilt, One Patch with fringe, maker unknown, ca. 1800, collection of Helen Foresman Spencer Museum of Art, University of Kansas, Lawrence (catalogued 28.914)
3. Helen Foresman Spencer Museum of Art, QUILTER'S CHOICE, Lawrence, KS, 1978, p. 10
4. Pieced Quilt, Medallion with Eight-Point Star, signed "Elizabeth Hart, Warwick Bucks Co., Penn., 1848." Collection of Helen Foresman Spencer Museum of Art, University of Kansas, Lawrence (catalogued 28.916)
5. Helen Foresman Spencer Museum of Art, QUILTER'S CHOICE, p. 6
6. Shankel, p. 62

7. Letha Rice, MADAM CARRIE A. HALL, Paper given at Kansas Quilt Symposium, Lawrence, 1978
8. Carrie A. Hall and Rose G. Kretsinger. THE ROMANCE OF THE PATCHWORK QUILT IN AMERICA, Caldwell, ID, 1935, p. 7
9. Hall and Kretsinger, p. 7
10. Letter, Carrie Hall to Minnie Moodie, January 15, 1938
11. Scrapbooks of Carrie Hall in the collection of the Helen Foresman Spencer Museum of Art, University of Kansas, Lawrence
12. Autobiography of Carrie Hall, manuscript in collection of Kansas State Historical Society, Topeka
13. Ibid.
14. Hall and Kretsinger, p. 7
15. Letter, Hall to Moodie, January 15, 1938
16. Pieced and appliqued quilt, George Washington Bi-Centennial, made by Carrie Hall, 1932, Leavenworth, KS. In collection of Helen Foresman Spencer Museum of Art, University of Kansas, Lawrence (catalogued 00.39)
17. Letter, Hall to Moodie, January 15, 1938
18. Jean Mitchell, QUILT KANSAS!, Lawrence, KS, 1978, p. 38
19. Betty Flack (ed.), LITTLE 'N BIG, Shumway, IL, 1964-66
20. Glenna Boyd (ed.), AUNT KATE'S QUILTING BEE, Burlson, TX and Vinita, OK, 1962-
21. Arlene Klindt (ed.), HOBBIES, CRAFTS AND QUILT NEWS, Maryville, MO, 1962-63
22. Mitchell
23. Barbara Brackman, AN ENCYCLOPEDIA OF PIECED QULT PATTERNS, Lawrence, KS, 1979-82
24. CRAFT HORIZONS, Vol. XXVI, No. 3, Cover

FOR FURTHER READING

Barbara Brackman "Madam Carrie Hall," QUILTER'S NEWS-LETTER MAGAZINE, #133, June, 1981

A Record of a Woman's Work —
The Betsey Reynolds Voorhees Collection

Mary Antoine de Julio

There has always been an interest in American needlework. Women have wanted to know what other women made, so the quilts, the bed hangings, and the samplers were collected. The fascination often centered on the antiquity of the textile or its historic association. Many times the pieces of needlework were preserved in a vacuum, with little information as to their age or creator.

Recent scholarship in American needlework has progressed greatly beyond these early efforts. Textiles are now studied in relationship to a whole. They are accurately identified, doing away with some of the historic romance associated with pieces. The needlework made by women is viewed as part of an entire period of style and living. Observations and research have led to conclusions as to regional designs and trends in needlework. Patterns and forms of stitchery are being attributed to schools.

Although these studies are thorough, many of the textiles are still researched out of context. Types of textiles are looked at relative to identical textiles — quilts to quilts, mourning pictures to mourning pictures. While this research has its place, a fact is often overlooked. Women did not make just one or two things; they made a "variety of domestic articles."[1] The questions who were the women who stitched these pieces, what all did they make, and how the one piece pertains to the whole of their ability often remain unanswered.

The study of the scope of a woman's ability and productivity

Mary A. de Julio is Director of the Montgomery County Historical Society, Fort Johnson, NY. Her address is: RD 1, Box 239 A1A, Pattersonville, NY 12137.

within the field of needlework is hampered. Textiles wear out over
the years, get thrown away, or are dispersed. Women did not keep
record books on the needlework they made, such as a cabinetmaker
would have, because their work was not for sale. Any personal notebooks that might contain information on what a woman did were
easily discarded as unimportant. Therefore, when one woman's work
is preserved, a rich source of data is available. The collection can be
examined and studied in relationship to its creator, but it can be a
mirror to an era. The Betsey Reynolds Voorhees Collection is such a
resource. Its size and the variety of objects within it can be the basis
for many studies on the entire spectrum of needlework made by
American women in the first half of the nineteenth century.

A grouping of approximately 170 pieces, the Betsey Reynolds
Voorhees Collection contains artwork, needlework, letterbooks, and
notebooks made by Betsey between 1800 and 1855. A woman of
character and determination, she began work while in school and
continued sewing and drawing through her married life, while
raising four sons and involving herself in social issues of the time.
Highly revered by her family, much of Betsey's art and needlework
was saved from sale and oblivion by her youngest son and, subse-
quently, his daughter. In 1917 the Collection was given to the Montgomery County Historical Society, Fort Johnson, New York, which
has preserved it since.

The Collection was always highly praised, but more for its association with a remarkable lady and her ancestors than for what it
contained. The time has come to look at the Collection and the
objects within it. They reveal much about Betsey Reynolds Voorhees, but the drawings, the textiles, the needlework and the notebooks can also disclose much about Betsey's contemporaries.

Betsey Reynolds was born December 9, 1790, the second of three
children of Dr. Stephen and Lydia Bartlett Reynolds. Though resid-
ing in Montgomery County, New York, Betsey's mother was from
Connecticut, and Dr. Reynolds had studied with a family friend in
that colony. Probably for these reasons, Betsey was sent to Litchfield, Connecticut for her education. Family tradition held that she
studied at Miss Sarah Pierce's Academy.[2] Though there is no record
of her attending Miss Pierce's school,[3] one of Betsey's notebooks includes a list of "Expenses while at Lichfield [sic]"[4] and two notebooks
contain compositions written while in that village.[5]

By 1810 Betsey was home in Minaville. On April 24, 1811 she married Dr. Samuel Voorhees. A young man from the neighboring town, Samuel had been studying medicine under Betsey's father. About 1820, they moved across the Mohawk River to the growing village of Amsterdam. They had purchased an imposing and already historic house on Main Street. Here Dr. Voorhees opened an office. Samuel and Betsey had three sons by the time they moved and a fourth was born in 1826. The Voorheeses maintained a position of respect in Amsterdam society. Their home contained furniture associated with historic personages. Dr. Voorhees put in a garden and hothouses in which he grew an assortment of fruits, vegetables, and flowers. After Betsey's death, the house and its furnishings, including Betsey's needlework, became somewhat of a museum. They remained in the Voorhees family until the early twentieth century.

Betsey's mother was a woman of artistic ability and perhaps from her Betsey learned the rudiments of stitchery. Her schooling also included instructions in needlework, for the list of "Expenses..." includes lace, Ribland [sic], skeins of silk, skeins of floss thread, flannel, and pelin [sic].[6] Her accomplishments with the needle were displayed at an early age. Betsey's granddaughter told the story that, when a girl of seventeen, Betsey "attended the county fair in Johnstown, attired from head to foot in garments manufactured by herself from the raw material, to her shoes, gloves and ribbons, and her straw hat was braided by her own deft fingers."[7] While this sounds like proud embellishment, if one looks at the Collection and the caliber of the textiles and knows from other records what else Betsey made, one is inclined to accept the granddaughter's story.

Like most girls, Betsey must have made items in preparation for her wedding. Only one piece remains, a candlewick coverlet. Made of two pieces of ribbed cotton, seamed down the center, Betsey embroidered a pattern of french knots and bullion stitch. The center motif is an urn filled with slender flowers. It is surrounded by a border of diamonds, then a border on three sides of swags and tassels. In making the coverlet, Betsey began a practice which has proven invaluable for research. The coverlet is dated 1811 and signed across the top BETSEY REYNOLDS.[8]

About thirty years later Betsey made another candlewick coverlet. Stitched on a heavy twill cotton, the coverlet is signed and dated

B.R. Voorhees 1844. It too has a center urn of flowers. There is a
wide border of suns, each having a flower in the center. Though
essentially the same pattern, there is a subtle difference. The pattern
in the 1844 coverlet is heavy and massive in feeling, while the earlier
piece looks light and airy. This difference could be accounted for by
the change in styles in thirty years. It could also have been caused by
areas of influence. Betsey had just returned from Connecticut when
she made the 1811 coverlet. By 1844 she had lived steadily in New
York over thirty-five years. There is a variance in New York inter-
pretation of styles. These two coverlets could be examples of this
difference.[9]

There is only one quilt in the collection. It is made with a fine cotton front and a loosely-woven linen back. The filling is cotton. The
three layers are attached with very fine stitching and, after the
design was completed, cotton was used to stuff the figures. In making
the quilt, a pattern was planned similiar in design to the two coverlets. The center medallion is a pomegranate, sprouting flowers and
palm leaves filled with hearts. This is surrounded by a double border
of running feather vine with flowers between. Around this is a wide
border of sunflowers and grapes flowing from cornucopias, and more
pomegranates and large flat leaves with hearts in their centers. At
the top of the quilt are two sunflowers. There is a set of initials in the
center of each flower—BRV and LR. The first initials obviously
stand for Betsey.The other two letters could be for Betsey's mother,
Lydia Reynolds, or for one of Betsey's three nieces each of whose
name began with L. No matter for whom the quilt was made, it is a
beautiful piece incorporating quilting and stuffing, which measures
89½ inches by 94½ inches.[10] (Figure 1)

The duties of motherhood did not stop Betsey from sewing. She
made many articles of clothing for herself and her sons. While many
women may have been satisfied sewing fine, well-tailored outfits, this
was not so for Betsey. Each piece that has been preserved contains
exquisite embellishments. The decorative designs and stitchery exhibit careful thinking and execution, and can tell students of the
1820 to 1840 period what women were sewing.

Betsey made much of her own clothing for daily use. Even the
smallest and most utilitarian pieces contain a diversity of decorative
stitches. A collar is embroidered with dyed linen thread and includes

Fig. 1. White cotton stuffed quilt, c. 1820–1840. Made by Betsey Reynolds Voorhees. Cat. #247, Montgomery County Historical Society.

netted lace flowers.[11] Aprons are enhanced with satin-stitched cornucopias or french-knotted grapes, leaves and tatting.[12] There are also
capes, shawls, and flannel wrappers. Each is enriched with inset lace,
embroidery, or tambour work.[13]

There are five vests in the Collection made by Betsey for her
sons. A red velvet and a cotton canvas vest are each embroidered in
small satin stitch flowers down the front and on the pockets. A
man's vest in striped wool flannel is covered in tambour work. Following the horizontal stripes, there are rows of Greek keys alternating with rows of stylized flowers. Two white cotton twill vests are
decorated with freehand ink drawing. Even the small covered

buttons have a flower sketched on them. Each vest is signed. One
was made for James, the other for Stephen, two of Betsey's sons.[14]
    While sending some clothes to her eldest son, Betsey wrote this
poem.

For you my fancy and my skill I tried
For you my needle with delight I plied
The work 'tho humble you will please to take
And wear it grateful for your mothers *sake*[15]

Pieces of children's clothing made for other relatives are part of the
Collection. Each is embroidered in a variety of stitches in white on
white or has ink highlights.

    When first looking at the ink decorated clothing, a hasty con-
clusion could be drawn that the flowers, hearts, and Greek keys are
embroidery patterns never used. A closer examination of the patterns and the quality of the drawing dispels that thought. The
designs are too detailed and fine, and in some cases include names or
words. Ink sketching was obviously a method of enhancing clothing.
An analysis of a linen handkerchief substantiates that conclusion.

    A large linen handkerchief made by Betsey is one of the most
fascinating pieces in the Collection. A wide border of what looks like
lace makes one wonder whether it was drawn or a method like silk
screening was employed to produce the effect. The center square is
more intriguing. Betsey sketched a portrait in three of the corners—
George Washington, Henry Clay, and Zachary Taylor. Under each
is the man's signature. In the fourth corner is an eagle with the
legend "To Stephen R. Voorhees—From his Mother—".[16] The
handkerchief proves that drawing was an acceptable decoration for
textiles. The handkerchief also demonstrates that while Betsey
sewed out of love for her family, much of the work was done for her
own pleasure and self-expression. Stephen R. Voorhees, for whom
the handkerchief was made, was blind.

    Betsey's feelings on needlework were aptly expressed in a letter to
a cousin.

It [needlework] is in fact but a species of painting where the
needle is used instead of the brush to diffuse the shade. In
ancient Rome tho the fine arts were considered to be under
the superintendance of Apollo and the Muses, yet painting

was by them particularly appropriated to Minerva there by uniting the qualities of wisdom with that of genius, and joining with most finished dexterity of art the more profound sagacity of science—[17]

Her dexterity of art practiced with a needle was to blossom in the next decade.

The reorganization of the New York State Agricultural Society in 1841 provided for an annual state fair and encouraged each county to institute their own fair.[18] These state and county fairs provided a vehicle for Betsey to display her fine needlework. In 1846 at the age of fifty-five Betsey won her first awards at the Montgomery County fair and was to continue entering and winning premiums until 1854.[19] The articles made for and displayed at the county and state fairs show the wide variety of needlework made by Betsey and other women during these years. Awards were given to Betsey for such items as woolen blankets, an embroidered cravat, stockings knit from linen, cotton, wool, and worsted wool, a Cott coverlid [sic], woolen coverlid, woolen carpets, suspenders, and table covers.[20] The list is numerous. Some of these articles are in the Collection with their entry cards.

"1 Pair Rose Blankets Woolen" displayed at a state fair is one of the finest examples of rose blankets. This type of blanket had been made in the eighteenth century, and these thick, richly embroidered samples indicate that their production continued into the mid-nineteenth century.[21]

A set of four folding cards were put together for display at a fair. Glued to both sides of the panels of each card are samples of tied cotton fringe. Some are missing, but there are over forty pieces of fringe, no two alike.[22]

The American Institute in New York City held annual fairs for the exhibition of domestic and machine-made goods. Betsey displayed some of her needlework at the Institute in at least 1844 and 1855. She made copious notes on her trip to the 1844 exhibition, including a list of eighty-nine articles she displayed.[23] It is no surprise that she won a silver cup "For the greatest variety of Household Manufacturers."[24] The list includes articles similar to those Betsey showed at the county fairs, but there were many different pieces. The list encompassed such items as "1 Cambrick Quilt, 1 printed

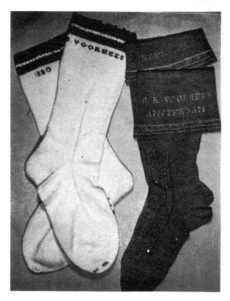

Fig. 2. Pair knit wool stockings signed and dated B. Voorhees 1820. Cat. #1373.
Pair knit tan linen stockings signed B R VOORHEES AMSTERDAM EX-
CELSIOR, c. 1840–1850. Cat. #1387, Montgomery County Historical
Society.

shirt and belt, 1 Knit Comfort, 1 Emb. Table cover w. beed, 1 pr. of Braceletts, 1 pr of mittens, and 1 wg chair cover."[25]

Some of the needlework can be dated because of some of the stories associated with them. In 1825 the Marquis de Lafayette toured the United States. His reception in Amsterdam was very poorly planned and few of the residents turned out to greet Lafayette. Betsey wrote to him in 1828, apologizing for her neighbors, and enclosed a pair of stockings she had knitted.[26] A similar pair of stockings, a fabric book in which she stitched a Lafayette ribbon, and a cross-stitched punch card envelope of Lafayette's thank you are thereby datable to 1828.[27] (Figure 2)

A plowing match was held at each county fair. Dr. Voorhees entered several of the first matches. Then in 1852 the Agricultural Society sponsored a special competition for "The old men...", which Samuel Voorhees entered. For the event Betsey made him a

Fig. 3. Linen smock with embroidery, 1852. Made by Betsey Reynolds Voorhees. Cat. #1107, Montgomery County Historical Society.

smock of homespun linen.[28] (Figure 3) The tatted lace edging and four large hearts she embroidered on the corners of the collar made the smock far superior to a farmer's shirt. Whether it was the smock or a "stiff Milk punch" which spurred him on, Dr. Voorhees won the match over two professional farmers.[29,30]

The Collection contains many more items, all of which provide a source of reference on the wide spectrum of needlework from the first half of the nineteenth century. Some of the artwork in the Collection reflects trends found in needlework, thereby giving more material for study.

Betsey Reynolds Voorhees was a remarkable lady, as many of her friends testified.[31] Whether her ability and her work were outstanding for the time or only comparable to what all women were doing has yet to be determined. The existence of this Collection supplies a basis for this and much further research.

Notes and References

1. Silver medal "Awarded to Mrs. B.R. Voorhees for choice variety of domestic articles.", in 1847, 329b; Betsey Reynolds Voorhees Collection, Montgomery County Historical Society.
2. Accession records; Montgomery County Historical Society, Fort Johnson, New York. Entry for 1917.
3. Emily Noyes Vanderpoel, CHRONICLES OF A PIONEER SCHOOL FROM 1792–1833, BEING THE HISTORY OF MISS SARAH PIERCE AND HER LITCHFIELD SCHOOL, University Press, Cambridge, Mass., 1903.
   Emily Noyes Vanderpoel, MORE CHRONICLES OF A PIONEER SCHOOL FROM 1792–1833, BEING ADDED HISTORY ON THE LITCHFIELD FEMALE ACADEMY KEPT BY MISS SARAH PIERCE AND HER NEPHEW, JOHN PIERCE BRACE, University Press, Cambridge, Mass., 1927.
4. BETSEY REYNOLDS.—POETRY. EXTRACTS., 199; Betsey Reynolds Voorhees Collection, MCHS.
5. Ibid; Betsey Reynolds Notebook 1807, 366; Betsey Reynolds Voorhees Collection, MCHS.
6. BETSEY REYNOLDS.—POETRY. EXTRACTS., 199; Betsey Reynolds Voorhees Collection, MCHS.
7. "Colonial Reception," THE DEMOCRAT, (Amsterdam, New York). February 23, 1904.
8. Document textile 247; MCHS.
9. Document textile 202: MCHS.
10. Document textile 247; MCHS
11. Document textile 351; MCHS.
12. Document textiles 1370; 1347; MCHS.
13. Document textiles 965; 964; 1105; 1103; MCHS.
14. Document textiles 1093; 1096; 1066; 1382; 1067; MCHS.
15. Letterbook of Betsey Reynolds Voorhees, Betsey Reynolds Voorhees Collection, MCHS. Entry dated February 7, 1834.
16. Document textile 1381; MCHS.
17. Letterbook of Betsey Reynolds Voorhees, Betsey Reynolds Voorhees Collection, MCHS. Entry circa 1835.

18. TRANSACTIONS OF THE NEW YORK STATE AGRICUL-TURAL SOCIETY WITH AN ABSTRACT OF THE PROCEED-INGS OF THE COUNTY AGRICULTURAL SOCIETIES; AND OF THE AMERICAN INSTITUTE, C. Van Benthysen & Co., Albany, N.Y., 1841–1846.

19. Secretary's Book of the Montgomery County Agricultural Society, 582; MCHS, Fort Johnson, New York.

20. Ibid.

21. Document textiles 1090a; 1090b; MCHS.

22. Document textiles 1112a–d; MCHS.

23. Notebook of Betsey Reynolds Voorhees, Betsey Reynolds Voorhees Collection, MCHS. Entries for September, 1844.

24. Silver cup "Awarded by the American Institute at the 17th Annual Fair 1844 to Mrs. B.R. Voorhees...", Betsey Reynolds Voorhees Collection, MCHS.

25. Notebook of Betsey Reynolds Voorhees, Betsey Reynolds Voorhees Collection, MCHS.

26. Betsey Reynolds Voorhees to the Marquis de Lafayette, Amsterdam, New York, September 4, 1828, A.L.S., Betsey Reynolds Voorhees Collection, MCHS.

27. Document textiles 999; 1345; 348; MCHS.

28. Document textile 997; MCHS.

29. "A Forceful Woman of the Days of Long Ago," SEMI-WEEKLY RECORDER DEMOCRAT, (Amsterdam, New York), June 24, 1917, p. 8.

30. Secretary's Book of MCAS.

31. Autograph book of Betsey Reynolds Voorhees 1828–1854, Betsey Reynolds Voorhees Collection, MCHS.

Fifteen Dearborn Quilts

Margaret Malanyn

The Dearborn, Michigan Historical Museum was established from two surviving buildings that were once part of a federal arsenal built in the 1830s. The Museum has acquired 120 quilts since the early 1950s, donated mainly by local citizens. Through a 1979–80 research grant from the American Association of University Women, the collection was recently studied, photographed and appraised.[1]

The quilt collection covers a time span ranging from the early 1800s through the Bicentennial and shows the great variety of work that quiltmakers did as the nation grew. Fifteen representative examples were selected for this study to demonstrate the way in which historical events were reflected in the quilts women made. Each quilt is numbered and arranged in chronological order with a brief description and explanation of its history included.

After the Revolutionary War the Great Lakes region was the first virgin territory inland to be settled and became known at that time as the Northwest Territory. It was filled with dense forests and thousands of lakes. Indians camped along streams and traveled largely by canoe. In 1807 the Territorial Governor and Chiefs of the Ottawas, Chippewas, Potawatomis and Hurons signed a treaty ceding a large area of southeast Michigan to the United States. In 1825 the Territory began to boom when the Erie Canal was opened and immense numbers of people traveled by water, up the canal to Buffalo and then by steamer across Lake Erie to Detroit.

The oldest quilt in the collection reflects the beginnings of the Dearborn area.

Margaret Malanyn is an artist and quiltmaker with a deep interest in women's needle arts. Her address is: 2601 Pelham Road, Dearborn, MI 48124.

Quilt #1—Star of Bethlehem pieced quilt, measuring 84" x 86", dates from the first quarter of the 19th century. It is all handmade of assorted cotton prints. Some of the prints, dating from the 18th century, have disintegrated.[2] A six-inch wide border encloses the large central star. The quilt backing is made from four 24-inch widths of brown cotton print material seamed together. Feather wreath designs are quilted into the four corners with diagonal lines spaced ⅜-inch apart used as background. Both light and dark quilting threads are used throughout. The quilt is finished with a narrow red and white printed cotton binding and is in excellent condition considering its age.

The elaborate quilt most likely was completed in New York state before 1830 when the style was popular.[3] It was carried to Michigan by the pioneering Richard Haigh family when they traveled up the Erie Canal in the early 1850s, according to Florence Haigh Richard, great-granddaughter of the maker.[4]

In 1835 the first railroad in the Territory, named the Detroit and St. Joseph R.R., was built across the southern part of the state to the eastern shore of Lake Michigan. By 1836 as many as 2,000 people were arriving by ship in a single day. As they traveled on they found dense forests of splendid timber, flocks of wild turkeys and large herds of deer roaming the woods. Bears were plentiful but not considered dangerous except to livestock. Log cabins were quickly built and land was cleared making islands of civilization in the vast wilderness. Schools were established with fall, winter and spring terms. Young children attended all three terms but older boys, whose labor was needed on the farms, only attended winter terms.

Michigan became a state in 1837. When the 1850 Constitution was adopted women were given the right to use or dispose of their own property without the consent of their husbands. In spite of demands for equal educational opportunities university admittance for women was denied until 1870. It was widely believed at that time that intellectual pursuits would damage women's brains.

Two appliqued quilts dating from the second quarter of the 19th century demonstrate the custom of the time when well-brought-up young ladies, using their choicest material and their best needlework, made their bridal quilt as soon as they were engaged to be married.[5]

Quilt #2—Rose of Sharon appliqued quilt, measuring 82" x 82",
c. 1840, is all handmade and has been preserved in excellent condition. Shades of pink, red, yellow and green calico prints are used to
applique flower and leaf shapes onto a white cotton background.
The quilt design is composed of four great square blocks of applique
surrounded with a meandering vine border.[6] The appliqued border
flowers are attached with buttonhole stitches.

The quilt donor, Mrs. Arley (Esther) Meeker, preserved and
cared for the quilt for sixty years. It descended from her husband's
side of the family. Named Rynearson, the family worked for the railroad from its beginning and lived in Buchanan, Michigan near the
eastern shore of Lake Michigan.[7]

Quilt #3—Rose of Sharon pieced and appliqued quilt, measuring
89" x 100", is dated between 1840-60. It is all handmade from calico
prints then known as oiled calicos[8] of red, pink, yellow and green
appliqued to a white background. The original colors have faded,
especially the green color which varies from pea green to blue-green.
The basic pattern is a foundation rose pieced from yellow, red and
pink calico and appliqued to a 13-inch white cotton square with
green leaves and buds added. Thirty blocks complete the quilt center
and are enclosed by a 12-inch wide border of pink and green buds
and leaves. Pale blue and white thread is used for the fine quilting
stitches made in a diamond pattern with lines spaced ½-inch apart
over the quilt surface. The backing is made from three 30½-inch
widths of coarse white cotton. The quilt is bound in red tape.[9]

Mrs. Davis, who appraised the entire quilt collection in April,
1980, stated that it was "an excellent bridal quilt."[10]

Another quilt, made in Tennessee and donated to the Dearborn
Museum by a great-granddaughter, shows the quality and artistry of
mid-century American quiltmaking and gives a glimpse into the
quiltmaker's life.

Quilt #4—Rolling Star pieced quilt, measuring 72" x 78½",
was made in 1847.[11] It is all handmade of an assortment of cotton
prints, now badly faded. The 36 eight-pointed star blocks are
arranged in a checkerboard pattern and surrounded by a Wild
Goose Chase border, also badly faded. A narrow brown and white
striped binding finishes the quilt edges. The backing is made from
four 23-inch widths of coarse white cotton. The quilting stitches are

very fine showing ten stitches to the inch and rows are spaced ⅝-inch apart. The quilt is in a worn out condition and only the stitches are holding it together.

The quiltmaker, Isabelle Simerly McKeehan, made the quilt when she was 54 years old.[12] She was born in the small village of Oak Grove, Tennessee in 1793. She married at age 27 and lived to be 102 years old. She was from a family of Irish farmers and all of her female descendents were considered fine quilters.

During the 1880s the former powder magazine of the Dearborn Federal Arsenal was converted to living quarters by Nathaniel and Elizabeth Ross. The home was used as a boarding house for many years and a cache of quilts was found when the house became a museum seventy years later. A Cross and Crown quilt was found among a fine assortment of patchwork quilts.

Quilt #5—Cross and Crown or Goose Tracks pieced quilt, measuring 70″ x 78″, c. 1850, is all handmade from red and white cotton fabric and shows no signs of wear. The solid red cotton color used in the patchwork and borders varies in color strength and most probably was home dyed.[13] Wide lattice strips separate the thirty blocks and help turn the pattern into a bold design. The backing is made from flour and sugar sacks with a stamped design from BB & R Knight, Providence, R.I., still visible on one of the sacks. The quilt is finished off with a white binding (Figure 1).

When the Museum was begun in the early 1950s a rare and out-standing quilt was donated. Little is known about its origin.

Quilt #6—all-white Stuffed Quilt, measuring 82″ x 90″, c. 1850, is made of fine quality white cotton. Four pieces of material, varying in widths from 15 to 20 inches, are seamed together to make up the top piece. An elaborate center design features a shield and banner with the motto "E Pluribus Unum" lettered inside. Thirteen stars are arranged above the banner. A classical egg and dart border encloses the central design. Flower-filled cornucopias and lyres with elaborate scrolls are worked into the outside borders. All of these intricate motifs are stuffed from the back where many slits have been cut, stuffing inserted and then the fabric has been closed with tiny stitches. The entire surface is quilted every half inch in a diamond pattern giving an overall puckered appearance. Narrow twill tape is used to finish the edges. This rare quilt has been preserved in near perfect condition.

During the quilt appraisal[14] Mrs. Davis suggested that the quilt may have come from the South because of its size and because a Southern lady would have had the time, money and skill to devote to such a project. She further commented that there was a strongly held belief by some Southerners before the Civil War that the Union should be preserved and that the quilt could very well be expressing that sentiment. A similar quilt, named a Secession Quilt, made in 1860 by Mrs. P.C. Cook of South Carolina, used some of the same ideas.[15]

As the Civil War approached there was much sentiment for the Union cause in Michigan, far removed from the South. Military units formed at the arsenal in 1859 when most of the area was still largely a wilderness.

Another historically significant quilt to the Dearborn area was given in 1957 by a great-granddaughter of a pioneering family.

Quilt #7—Autographed Album Quilt, measuring 66" x 81", is all handmade. Thirty blocks, each pieced from a different calico print, contain the names of friends, relatives and neighbors of the Morris Halsted family written in indelible ink. White lattice strips, measuring 3½ inches wide, frame and separate the blocks. The quilt is backed with three pieces of coarse white cotton material seamed together. It is finished with a narrow green binding. A quilted clam shell pattern appears in the blocks, flower and leaf patterns are used to quilt the lattice strips and a maple leaf pattern is quilted in the borders (Figure 2).

Morris Halsted of New York state built a log cabin in the area in 1837. He then returned to New York, married Delaney Vanostrand in 1839 and together they traveled to Michigan where they home-steaded. A son Chauncey was born in 1840. Records show[16] that Chauncey enlisted in the Volunteers of Co. D, 6th Michigan Infantry, Heavy Artillery, during the Civil War and was home on leave in the spring of 1864 when the quilt was made.[17] All who auto-graphed the quilt were early settlers in the area. Chauncey's name appears in the top center row with friends' names grouped on either side. Close relatives' names are arranged in the second row with his grandparents' names inverted, the only signatures positioned that way on the quilt. Neighbors' and other friends' names are arranged in the remaining rows below. Perhaps the quilt was made for

Chauncey as an expression of friendship from those closest to him.[18]
He returned to duty and died in August, 1864 at Vicksburg.

After the Civil War the need for the Dearborn arsenal was gone
and it was closed in 1872. As the frontier moved rapidly westward
many veterans were encouraged to take up land in the prairie states.
A popular quilt pattern of the day had evolved through many name
changes. Originally called Job's Tears in colonial times, it was re-
named Kansas Troubles or Rocky Road to Kansas after the Civil
War.[19]

Quilt #8—Rocky Road to Kansas pieced and tied comforter,
measuring 72½" x 79", c. 1870, is all handmade. Thirty blocks are
pieced from a fine variety of multi-colored cotton material and set in
lattice strips. The backing is seamed together from assorted sized
pieces of cotton prints. A thick filler is held in place with tied yarns
every few inches. A whisker guard is basted over the top edge of
the quilt.

The comforter, found in the Ross House, has been attributed to
Elizabeth Ross whose husband Nathaniel had a formidable beard.
She must have resorted to sewing extra material along the top edge
of her quilt to protect her fine handiwork from an oily and abra-
sive beard.

Quilt #9—Hexagon pieced quilt, measuring 75" x 77", c. 1880, is
all hand pieced from tan and red cotton and unbleached muslin.
The large sized hexagon pieces are arranged in a diagonally striped
pattern. The borders, measuring 5 inches wide, are cut too short and
are pieced out with extra material. They are machine stitched to the
center patchwork. The unbleached muslin backing has machine
stitched seams. A thin filler has been added and is quilted in a scalloped pattern. Quilting stitches are uneven, with many large sized
stitches showing and visible thread endings. Spacing between
quilting lines is irregular. The binding is machine stitched. The quilt,
found in the Ross House, is clearly the work of a beginner[20] and has
been attributed to Elizabeth Ross's daughter, Ellen Ramsey Ross,
who died of tuberculosis at age fifteen.[21]

During the last quarter of the 19th century the growth of the
needlework industry afforded women the opportunity to become
even more creative in an art form that was uniquely their own. A
wide variety of art needlework was made at that time to demonstrate

Fig. 1.Detail, <u>Cross and Crown</u> *pieced quilt, 70" x 78". #RB-12, Courtesy the Dearborn Historical Commission.*

the quiltmaker's skill.

Quilt #10—<u>Flower Basket</u> appliqued and stuffed quilt, measuring 63" x 79", c. 1880, is made of silk and wool fabrics in shades of red, orange and green. A flower-filled basket is appliqued to a dark, neutral background, with white touches adding accent to the unique design. Some of the flowers are stuffed. Other flowers and leaves are arranged around the central basket. The backing is seamed by machine. Fine hand quilting is made in a diamond pattern. The quilt is bound in narrow red wool applied by machine.

The quiltmaker, Sarah Gardner, lived in the Dearborn area and nursed her ailing mother until her death in 1880. Sarah married William Leslie in 1882 when she was 32 years old and he was 50 years old. In an old photograph Sarah is shown standing beside her seated husband wearing her dark green silk wedding dress, purchased by selling the family cow according to Mahala Brown, the quiltmaker's daughter.[22] Some of her applique needlework embellishes the bodice and sleeves of the dress, which is in the museum's costume collection.

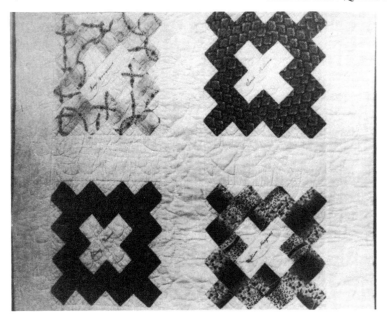

Fig. 2. Detail, Autographed pieced quilt, 66" x 81". #57-86.2, Courtesy the Dearborn Historical Commission.

Basket quilts were made all through the 19th century, although there was a sharp decline in all quiltmaking activities by the end of the century.[23]

Quilt #11—Basket pieced quilt, measuring 73" x 78½", c. 1890, is made of blue, brown and white cotton prints and is pieced by machine. Blue lattice strips surround each of the eighteen basket blocks which are set on point. The white cotton backing is made from three widths of material with machine stitched seams. Fine handstitches are used in the quilting design of leaves and flowers. A white binding is used to finish the quilt edges.

The quiltmaker, Mary Belle Sherer Haight, was born in 1872 in Branch County, southwest of Dearborn near the Indiana border. Her German ancestors first came to America in 1810. She made many quilts during her lifetime and quilted until only a few years before her death in 1957 according to her son Floyd Haight.[24]

Fig. 3. Quiltmakers of the Ladies' Aid Society, First Methodist Church, Dearborn, 1890. Courtesy the Dearborn Historical Commission.

Crazy quilts gained wide popularity during the 1870s, 80s and 90s and flourished until about 1910. Almost every home had one displayed in the parlor. As new materials were developed and existing supplies became cheaper and more widely available, more and more women learned to use their needlework skills to express their individuality in original designs, combinations of styles and pattern variations.[25]

Three examples from the Museum's collection of twenty Crazy quilts have been selected and studied because the most information was available about the quilts and the quiltmakers.

Quilt #12—Crazy Parlor Throw, measuring 63" x 76", dated 1891, is composed of thirty blocks made from fine quality velvets, silks and unusual fabrics and embellished with a variety of embroidery stitches. One of the center blocks is signed by Mrs. J.S. Walker, president of the Ladies' Aid Society of the First Methodist Church of Dearborn. The quilt was made for her, according to her granddaughter who was one of the donors.[26]

In an 1890 photograph taken at the church, members of the

Fig. 4. Detail, Crazy quilt, inscribed "H. Purdy" and 1892," 63" x 78".
#55-70, Courtesy the Dearborn Historical Commission.

Ladies' Aid Society posed with Mrs. Walker standing in the front
center row (Figure 3). The group continued to quilt for the church
for over fifty years. An article about quilts appearing in GRADUATE
WOMAN, the magazine of the American Association of University
Women, dated July, 1979, stated,

> In their heart of hearts, many Puritan women must have
> chafed at the stern rules set down and enforced by their dour
> menfolk. Their dress was demure, their lives beyond reproach,
> but rebellion shone in the quilts they made. The works of their
> hands sometimes bordered on sinful extravagance—not,
> heaven forbid, in monetary terms—but in fanciful design,
> joyous color and pride of execution.[27]

Quilt #13—A Crazy Quilt, measuring 63" x 78", is dated 1892
and is signed by the quiltmaker near the center. Thirty blocks, composed of assorted sized pieces of velvet and wool, are combined and

embellished with elaborate embroidery stitches. Some of the embroidery designs include flowers, animals, insects, monograms, canoes and fans which appear in two corners. The quilt is backed with maroon sateen and bound with maroon wool tape (Figure 4). The quiltmaker, Hattie Purdy, was born in the Dearborn area in 1862 and spent all of her 93 years there according to her son Charles Purdy.[28] Her quilt is a gay and happy memento of her life and its many activities when she was about 30 years old.

Quilt #14—Crazy buffalo robe, measuring 66" x 70", c. 1900, is made from woolen scrap pieces. Soft shades of red, orchid, green, gray, brown, black and white are combined in irregular patches with the initials F.H. designed in the center of the robe. A heavy ribbed and flowered material in shades of red and tan is used as a backing. Feather stitching is used to embellish the surface and the two layers are tied together.

During the first decade of the 20th century woolen material and buffalo robes were manufactured at the Arna Mill in Dearborn. Buffalo robes were used for autos, carriages and other transportation opened to the elements that required warm covers for passengers' comfort. The Arna Mill employed many local people, and was destroyed in a spectacular fire in 1910.[29]

By the beginning of the 20th century women no longer spent hours piecing quilt tops or devoted long hours bent over a quilt frame. They purchased and used manufactured goods with enthusiasm and pride. More and more women began to work outside the home. Most of them were young and single or widowed or divorced. Another quilt example was made by a woman from such circumstances.

Quilt #15--Dresden Plate appliqued and pieced quilt, measuring 83" x 98", is dated from the first quarter of the 20th century. Hand pieced multi-colored cotton prints form the "plates." These are appliqued by machine to a white foundation block. Yellow lattice strips separate the blocks. A 10-inch wide yellow and white, wedge-shaped border encloses the center blocks. Two large yellow pieces of cotton seamed together form the quilt backing. Yellow bias tape is used to finish the scalloped quilt edges. The intricate quilting is done by machine using matching thread, i.e., white on top and yellow on the quilt back. It is a really fine example of machine quilting with no visible thread tails.

The quiltmaker, Amanda Dietrick, was born in Wisconsin in 1869. She was an accomplished seamstress and taught art and weaving to Indian children in Steward, Nevada from 1915 to 1935 in the Indian Field Service. After her retirement she made her home in Dearborn with her sister, Mary Dietrick Haight, and brother-in-law, Floyd L. Haight, until her death in 1947.[30]

All through the 19th and 20th centuries quiltmaking reflected the changes that were taking place as the nation grew. New quilt-making ideas and names were swiftly spread by the westward movement of the population. Rapid industrialization, including the introduction of the sewing machine, lightened the work load and changed women's roles as many joined the work force. The art and skill of quiltmaking continued, producing new ideas, originality and experimentation in needlework.

Appendix — Quilts from the collection of the Dearborn Historical Museum, Dearborn, Michigan

Quilt #1—Star of Bethlehem pieced quilt—56-33.11
Quilt #2—Rose of Sharon appliqued quilt—80-2.2
Quilt #3—Rose of Sharon pieced and appliqued quilt—70-84.9
Quilt #4—Rolling Star pieced quilt—72-77
Quilt #5—Cross and Crown or Goose Tracks pieced quilt—RB-12
Quilt #6—All-white Stuffed Quilt—53-63.4
Quilt #7—Autographed Album quilt—57-86.2
Quilt #8—Rocky Road to Kansas pieced and tied comforter—RB-8
Quilt #9—Hexagon pieced quilt—RB-9
Quilt #10—Flower Basket appliqued and stuffed quilt—55-19.12
Quilt #11—Basket pieced quilt—71-104.10
Quilt #12—Crazy Parlor Throw—66-82
Quilt #13—Crazy Quilt—55-70
Quilt #14—Crazy buffalo robe—55-82
Quilt #15—Dresden Plate appliqued and pieced quilt—71-104.12

Notes and References:

1. Quilt Appraisal by Mary Kay Davis, Dearborn Historical Museum Records Library, Dearborn, MI. Taped comments recorded April, 1980.
2. Quilt Appraisal by Mary Kay Davis, DHM Records Library.
3. Patsy and Myron Orlofsky, QUILTS IN AMERICA, McGraw-Hill, New York, 1974, p. 301.
4. Margaret Malanyn, interview with Florence Haigh Richard, April, 1980.
5. Rose Wilder Lane, WOMAN'S DAY BOOK OF AMERICAN NEEDLEWORK, New York, 1963, p. 93.
6. Ruth Finley, OLD PATCHWORK QUILTS, Branford, Mass., 1970, pp. 125-127.
7. Malanyn, Interview with Mrs. Arley (Esther) Meeker, Dearborn, November, 1979 and April, 1980.
8. Orlofsky, p. 326.
9. Orlofsky, p. 257.
10. Quilt Appraisal by Mary Kay Davis, DHM Records Library
11. 1972 Accessions Record Book, DHM Records Library.
12. Malanyn, Interview with Iris Shaw, Dearborn, May, 1980.
13. Quilt Appraisal by Mary Kay Davis, DHM Records Library.
14. Quilt Appraisal by Mary Kay Davis, DHM Records Library.
15. Georgiana Brown Harbeson, AMERICAN NEEDLEWORK, Coward-McCann, 1938, pp. 36-37.
16. Records Book, 6th Michigan Infantry, Civil War 1861-65, Ihling Bros. and Everard, Kalamazoo, MI, 1904, p. 2, DHM Library.
17. 1957 Accessions Record Book, DHM Records Library.
18. Finley, pp. 189-193.
19. Orlofsky, p. 247.
20. Orlofsky, p. 60.
21. Dearborn Historical Records Library.
22. Malanyn, interview with Mrs. Howard (Mahala Gardner) Brown, Dearborn, November, 1979.
23. Orlofsky, p. 62.

24. Malanyn, interviews with Mr. Floyd Haight, Dearborn, November, 1979, June, 1980.

25. Orlofsky, pp. 290, 312.

26. 1966 Accessions Record Book, DHM Records Library.

27. Mary Abrams, "Quilting—An American Women's Art," GRADUATE WOMAN, July, 1979, p. 16.

28. 1955 Accessions Record Book, DHM Records Library.

29. DHM Records Library.

30. Malanyn, interviews with Mr. Haight.

The Quilts of Grant Wood's Family and Paintings

Mary Cross

In the summer of 1981 while visiting family in Iowa City, Iowa, I received an invitation to study the quilts of Grant Wood's family. The current owner, Edwin Green, a close personal friend and devotee of Wood, was seeking recommendations about their future location.

The two quilts in Iowa City were given to Green by Wood's sister Nan Wood Graham. They were made by Lydia Wood, Grant Wood's maiden great aunt. No birthdate is available at this time for Lydia Wood, but it is known that she was the third child born in her family. Wood's grandfather Joseph Wood was the first born in 1824. They were born in Springboro, Ohio.

The immigrant ancestor was Quaker Othiwell Wood, who was born in Lancaster, England, and came to America about 1731. He settled in Chester County, Pennsylvania.[1] The family line descended through Jesse and Hannah Hollingsworth Wood, Grant Wood's great grandparents. The family of Joseph and Rebecca Shepard Wood migrated to Iowa from Winchester, in the Shenandoah Valley, Virginia by covered wagon. They eventually settled on a farm three and one-half miles from Anamosa, Iowa, in the rolling hills of the Mississippi River Valley. Grant Wood's father Francis Maryville Wood married Hattie De Ette Weaver.[2] The Weaver family had migrated to Iowa from upstate New York in the 1840s. Francis Wood's maiden sister Sarah inherited the quilts from Aunt Lydia Wood, who had continued to live in Virginia. Nan Wood Graham, in turn, inherited them from Aunt Sarah Wood in 1919[3] (Figure 1).

Mary Cross is a quilt teacher and lecturer. Her address is: 805 NW Skyline Crest, Portland, OR 97229.

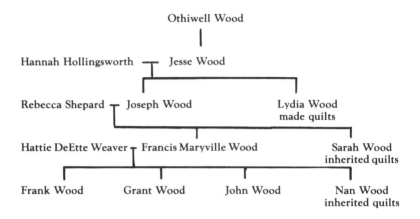

Othiwell Wood

Hannah Hollingsworth ┬ Jesse Wood

Rebecca Shepard ┬ Joseph Wood   Lydia Wood
                                                 made quilts

Hattie DeEtte Weaver ┬ Francis Maryville Wood   Sarah Wood
                                                       inherited quilts

Frank Wood   Grant Wood   John Wood   Nan Wood
                                                           inherited quilts

Fig. 1. The Wood family line.

The eight-pointed <u>Star</u> quilt is colonial bed size 102" x 106". It dates from between 1840–1860 in Ohio or Virginia. The condition is good considering the brown streak and the migration of one fabric's dye. There are forty-two star blocks and fifty-six white blocks. The finished size of the star is six inches. Each star is set in a brown fabric frame, giving a finished block size of 8¼ inches. This type of set called "cross-bar" was popular everywhere, especially with Pennsylvania women who liked to make striking contrasts between blocks.[4] The print fabrics have mostly brown fields with only one showing deterioration. One of the most outstanding features is the quality of the piecing. The fabrics have been joined in ways that make it extremely difficult to tell where the seams are located. The stars with more than one fabric show a very careful attention to fabric placement with matching pieces equally balanced forming the star points. The quilting is very intricate with six stitches per inch. The patterns are princess feather wreaths and either a pineapple or a cluster of grapes in the white blocks. A princess feather garland is quilted on the white border. In between, the rest of the quilting is gridwork. The backing is 32-inch wide "homespun." The knots show on the back of the quilt. The quilt has "Nan Wood 1919" written in pen in one corner. This was the date she inherited the quilt[5] (Figure 2).

Fig. 2. Eight-Pointed Star, 1840–1860, made by Lydia Wood. 102" x 106". Photo by author.

The second quilt is the Noonday or Sunburst pattern. "It was only natural that the early housewife's day was" marked "by the rising and setting of the sun. After dark, . . . only the most primitive (forms of) lighting . . . such as rushlight holders, phoebe or betty lamps, and candles," were available. "After 1812 whale oil for lamps became cheaper and more available." Kerosene lamps became the accepted light device after the fuel was approved for home use about 1860.[6] The overall size of the quilt is 107" x 108" indicating it was made for a large bed. This all-cotton quilt dates from the same 1840–1860 year period. The sixty-four 8½" finished circles are set in an elaborate and difficult to make arrangement according to Ruth Finley.[7] There are fifteen diamonds surrounding each circle. This motif is classified as solar variant in the design field and was derived from Japanese heraldry and Arabian sources.[8] The diamonds are repeated in double rows along the border of the entire quilt. The diamonds in the corners create arrowheads forming a nice solution to the corner treatment problem. The diamond segments were not cut consistently according to grain or design of the fabric. The end row of blocks are all the same fabric indicating (perhaps) that the quilter needed to add extra length or perhaps she ran out of the other fabrics. The quilting is magnificent. It consists primarily of garlands of princess feathers that wind around the circular blocks across the quilt's surface. The cotton batting has seeds in it. The backing is of consistent weave and thirty-six inch width. There is an "SS" stamped near the edge of the backing[9] (Figure 3).

The decision has been made to donate the quilts to the Living History Farms of Iowa near Des Moines. The plans are underway to construct a quilt house to serve as a center for antique textiles and research. When this building is completed, the quilts will be presented.

As I studied these quilts, I began to wonder if there were others available from the Wood family. I began to wonder about Grant Wood's artistic talents. Had he inherited his interest in meticulous detail work from the Wood family? Had he ever used these quilts or similar ones for any of his paintings? I was challenged and the research was started.

Grant Wood may not have known these quilts existed because, to Edwin Green's knowledge, they were never displayed at his home. Green would stay at the house while Wood traveled.[10]

To my delight, I learned there are at least four other quilts. One being Grant Wood's baby quilt. He gave it along with his combination cradle and youth bed to his Cedar Rapids, Iowa patron's wife Mrs. David Turner. The two items are now part of the John B. Turner Collection at the Cedar Rapids Art Center.

A Four-patch variation quilt was made by Grandmother Nancy Weaver for Grant, who was born February 13, 1891. The overall size is 31¼" x 34½". The 3¾" pieced and solid blocks create diagonal lines of color and texture across the quilt surface. The fifteen rows of blocks contain 21 different calicos and woven checks of the type dating from 1880-1900. There are purple and white, red and black, a red and white calico as well as brown and blue checks. One outside row is made of totally different fabrics causing a break in the flow of design and color. Speculation would be that either the quilter ran out of fabrics or needed to add extra width to the finished top. There is careful piecing of some of the blocks with most of the fabrics placed on the straight of grain and only one on the diagonal. There are 5

Fig. 3. Noonday or Sunburst, all cotton, 1840–1860, made by Lydia Wood. 107" x 108". Photo by author.

stitches per inch in the quilting lines that flow in parallels across the surface. The backing and binding are of a pink and white print. The quilt has been mounted and framed with glass for many years. The overall condition is good except for some fading. The batting is a smooth consistency of wool. There is one place where the quilting lines do not come through to the back[11] (Figure 4).

Three other quilts have been inherited by Nan Wood Graham. Two of them are stored in an old trunk which is unavailable at this time. One is an Album quilt made and signed by friends of Joseph Wood. The other, Mrs. Graham reports, is a colonial-sized quilt in poor condition but with evidence still of beautiful quilting. Further examination will depend upon the trunk becoming available from storage and the convenience for Mrs. Graham to study them. The third quilt is currently missing. It was consigned to an Arts Alliance shop at Riverside, California's historic Mission Inn. The quilt was sold to someone from the East who requested the shop get verification from Mrs. Graham. Unfortunately, the shop went bankrupt

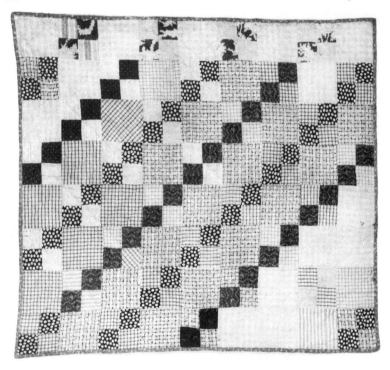

Fig. 4. *Four-Patch variation, made by Nancy Weaver circa 1891. 31¼" x 34½".
Grant Wood's baby quilt. Courtesy the Cedar Rapids Museum of Art, Gift of
Harriet Y. and John B. Turner, II.*

before she was able to get the buyer's name and to collect her profit
from the sale.[12]

To my further joy, I learned about two paintings done by Grant
Wood containing quilts. These I was able to track down through a
nationwide search of museums, researchers, and Grant Wood en-
thusiasts. A current complete listing of his works and their locations
does not exist. The first, "Quilts," was painted in 1928 and the
second, "Spring in Town," was painted in 1941. Further study of
Grant Wood's work led to the finding that these two oil paintings
clearly represented the two distinct styles of his work.

Fig. 5. Painting, "Quilts," Grant Wood, 1928. Courtesy James Sigmund.

The first quilt-related painting, "Quilts," was typical of the style he was using during the first part of his career. His familiar themes of trees, backyards, and simple structures are present (Figure 5).

The setting is a cottage next door to his friend's summer cottage in Waubeek, Iowa. The son of the cottage owner remembers Wood approaching Mrs. Miles, the neighbor lady, as she was airing her quilts, and asking permission to paint them. He remembers looking over Wood's shoulder as he painted. This memory was preserved by Wood through his techniques of narrowing the field of vision and of closing the composition. This creates an immediate presence as the viewer studies the quilts from a vantage point of standing on the road with the artist, just as the current owner did fifty-five years ago. The warmth of the colors shows the affection the artist and friends had for the location. Thus the painting has great personal meaning to the owner's family and has rarely been shared with the viewing public. It is not listed in any of the inventories of Wood's work except for an unauthorized 1941 publication which identified it as being part of an estate. It was given to Wood's host the moment it was completed and never went to his studio where, perhaps, it would have been formally recorded. The overall effect of the painting is an encounter with small-town life that appears to rarely change.[13]

Soon after completing the "Quilts" painting, Wood went to Munich, Germany to supervise the creation of a stained glass window for the Cedar Rapids Veterans' Memorial Coliseum. Visiting the annual exhibition at the Glass Palace, he was impressed by the Gothic painters, especially Memling, for their attention to detail and accuracy. Later, speaking with Irma Koen of the CHRISTIAN SCIENCE MONITOR, March 26, 1932, Wood stated:

> Until several years ago, I was strongly influenced by the Impressionistic school probably because I was taught to paint after their manner. However. my natural tendencies were toward the extremely detailed. As a boy, I once painted a picture of a bunch of currants which no one—not even a Japanese—could have executed with a more meticulous finish. At this period none of my work was ever accepted in any important exhibition.... It seemed to me the Gothic painters were the next step.... The lovely apparel and accessories of the Gothic period appealed to me so vitally that I longed to see pictorial and decorative possibilities in our contemporary clothes and art articles. Gradually as I searched, I began to realize that there was real decoration in the rickrack braid on the aprons of the farmers' wives, in calico patterns and in lace curtains. At present my most useful reference and one that is authentic is a Sears, Roebuck catalog. And so, to my great joy, I discovered that in the very commonplace, in my native surroundings, were decorative adventures and that my only difficulty had been in taking them for granted.[14]

Returning to Iowa, he developed his new direction which was to result in the creation of "American Gothic" in 1930 and its instant

Fig. 6. Oil painting, "Spring in Town," Grant Wood, 1941. 26" x 24½". Permanent collection, The Sheldon Swope Art Gallery, Terre Haute, IN.

fame and notoriety. The famous painting of the bald-headed villager and his daughter in front of a hybrid Gothic-style house won the Norman Wait Harris bronze medal and $300 purchase award at the Chicago Art Institute's Annual Exhibition of American Paintings. Wood became a prime favorite of Americans. His paintings were the most popular of American artists at the Chicago Century of Progress Exposition in 1933. Popularity with the public was important to him.

He wanted his work "to mean something to the public at large, not just a hypersensitive minority."[15]

Wood's choice was to depict the farmer as the possessor/caretaker of the land, as in his last quilt-related painting. In the summer of 1941, exhausted by pressures on him as a ranking artist, from the petty attacks on him by the public, and his own ill health, Wood spent the summer in Clear Lake, Iowa. Here, using an abandoned railroad depot as a studio, he created his last two oil paintings, "Spring in the Country" and "Spring in Town."

This second quilt-related painting, "Spring in Town," shows the sense of anticipation and preparation for the new season in the illustrated activities. From a vantage point above the scene, the viewer looks down as the young girl is pulling over the branch of spring blossoms and the woman is airing her quilts. This position gives the viewer the impression of looking into a make-believe scene. Wood often showed the woman's role to be that of beautifier and conservator. Man, on the other hand, is shown as the caretaker spading the garden, mowing the lawn, beating the rugs, and checking the roof after the long winter (Figure 6).

These represent his theme of man as the possessor of the land, carefully and lovingly working it to his benefit. However, these are not only Grant Wood themes, they are the traditional roles of rural Iowans. The picture of the small town church at a great distance from the city's factories and smokestacks shown in the distant corner of the painting is another tribute to the good life in rural Iowa. A further notion is that as long as man works his fields in harmony with nature, no harm will come to him and he will receive his material rewards. Wood considered both of his spring paintings of 1941 as patriotic statements in face of the approaching war. According to an interview in the CEDAR RAPIDS GAZETTE June 29, 1941, Wood described the paintings as representing the good life at stake, "inspired by a new appreciation of an America tranquil in a warring world, of democracy free and hopeful, of a country worth preserving."[16]

Although he may not have known the Wood family quilts existed and thus did not use them in his paintings, I conclude that Wood was probably attracted to the subject for his first painting, "Quilts," through his interest in carefully planned and detailed items in his environment. Quilts airing on the spring day are a natural example. In "Spring in Town," I conclude he used the quilts to illustrate woman's role as beautifier of her home through her artistic expressions. The airing quilts of both paintings are illustrative of his favorite theme—the beautiful, peaceful life available in American small towns.

Quilts
1. Pieced Quilt, Star, made by Lydia Wood, Virginia, Mid-19th century, in collection of Edwin Green
2. Pieced Quilt, Noonday or Sunburst, made by Lydia Wood, Virginia, mid-19th century, in collection of Edwin Green
3. Pieced Quilt, Four-patch variation, made by Nancy Weaver, Iowa, c. 1890, in John B. Turner collection at Cedar Rapids, Iowa Art Center
4. Pieced Quilt, unknown, in collection of Nan Wood Graham
5. Pieced Quilt, Album, in collection of Nan Wood Graham
6. Pieced Quilt, unknown

Notes and References:

1. Interview with Nan Wood Graham, October, 1982.
2. NATIONAL CYCLOPEDIA OF AMERICAN BIOGRAPHY, White and Co., 1949, Vol 35, p. 522.
3. Interview with Nan Wood Graham, November, 1982.
4. Ruth Finley, OLD PATCHWORK QUILTS, Branford, 1980, p. 131.
5. Interview.
6. Lilian Carlisle, PIECED WORK AND APPLIQUE QUILTS AT SHELBURNE MUSEUM, Shelburne Museum, Shelburne, VT, 1957, p. 16.
7. Finley, op. cit., p. 131.
8. Carlisle, op. cit., p. 34.
9. Pieced quilt, Noonday, made by Lydia Wood, c. 1840–1860, in the collection of Edwin Green.
10. Interview with Edwin Green, June, 1982.
11. Pieced quilt, Four-patch, made by Nancy Weaver, c. 1890, in the John B. Turner Collection at the Cedar Rapids Art Center.
12. Interview with Nan Wood Graham, October, 1982.
13. Interview with James Sigmund, June, 1982.
14. Quoted in Joan Liffring-Zug, THIS IS GRANT WOOD COUNTRY, Davenport Municipal Art Gallery, Davenport, Iowa, 1977, p. 27.
15. Edwin Green, "A Grant Wood Sampler," PALIMPSEST, State Historical Society of Iowa, Iowa City, January 1972, p. 14.
16. James Dennis, GRANT WOOD, Viking, 1975, p. 247.

Bibliography

Carlisle, Lilian Baker, PIECED WORK AND APPLIQUE QUILTS AT SHELBURNE MUSEUM, Shelburne Museum, Shelburne, VT, 1957

Dennis, James, "An Essay into Landscapes, the Art of Grant Wood," Kansas State University, Manhattan, Kansas, Fall, 1972, Vol. 4, No. 4

Dennis, James, GRANT WOOD, A STUDY IN AMERICAN ART AND CULTURE, Viking, 1975

Finley, Ruth, OLD PATCHWORK QUILTS AND THE WOMEN WHO MADE THEM, Branford, 1980

Garwood, Darrell, ARTIST IN IOWA: A LIFE OF GRANT WOOD, Norton, 1941

Green, Edwin, "A Grant Wood Sampler," PALIMPSEST, State Historical Society of Iowa, Iowa City, January, 1972

Liffring-Zug, Joan, THIS IS GRANT WOOD COUNTRY, Davenport Municipal Art Gallery, Davenport, Iowa, 1977

Interviews
Mr. Edwin Green of Iowa City, Iowa
Mr. and Mrs. James Sigmund of Solon, Iowa
Mr. John B. Turner of Cedar Rapids, Iowa
Mrs. Nan Wood Graham of Riverside, California
Mrs. Nadine Larson of Iowa City, Iowa

Museums and Galleries consulted
Minneapolis Institute of Art
Muskegon, Michigan Museum of Art
Sheldon Swope Gallery, Terre Haute, Indiana
Cedar Rapids Art Center, Cedar Rapids, Iowa

Marseilles Quilts and their Woven Offspring

Sally Garoutte

The French input to early American quilts has been surprisingly ignored. The relations between France and England's American colonies were very close in the late-colonial period, and one would expect to find some influences. The influences, however, came through England and so their origins have generally been lost. In the politics of that time (not too different from our own) France supported the American colonies in their bid for independence–while carrying on an extensive British trade.

For the most part England had the North American trade monopolized through control of colonial ports and import fees. Few French ships visited ports in America between the French islands in the Caribbean and eastern Canada. But English traders bought vast quantities of wine, and cotton and silk textiles from France, and transshipped great amounts to the Colonies, making their profit on the markup.

In the 17th and 18th centuries, France, England, Spain, Portugal and Holland were all vying for the trade routes of the world. At that time, the products shipped from the New World eastward to the Old World were nearly all raw materials in the form of lumber for shipbuilding, chemicals, food items such as fish and grain, fur for making hats, and of course tobacco. The products shipped westward from Europe were all finished consumer goods—textiles, furniture, nails, iron pots, tools, utensils, paper and books. By far the largest and most frequent shipments were of textiles of all kinds.

Textile production in those times in Europe was the most extensive kind of manufacture. Even the word "manufactures" was almost synonymous with textiles. (Our modern word "fabrics" means manufactures and is again almost synonymous with textiles.) It is

Sally Garoutte is a quilt historian with a strong interest in textile history. Her address is: 105 Molino Avenue, Mill Valley, CA 94941.

Fig. 1. Quilt from Provence in Museon Arletan, Arles, France. (New photo not available.)

difficult to comprehend the enormous place textiles once had, before fuels made engines possible. But there simply were not a lot of other man-made things in the world of that time except what people made for their own use. Most people who made things to sell made textiles in one form or another.

Among things made to sell in the 17th century in the area of southern France known as Provence, were quilts. Three of these 17th century quilts from Arles are in the collections of the Museon Arlaten, a folk art museum displaying the ancient crafts of Provence. Descriptions and photographs of the quilts were published in France in 1926 (Figure 1). Two of the quilts shown were all-white with elaborate stuffed and corded motifs. The third had a center of the type of printed cotton known as "indienne" quilted in double diamonds, surrounded by a border of plain dark cloth heavily quilted in what appears to be a floral design, and completed at the outer edges with several straight parallel rows quilted very close together—typical of all these quilts.[1]

The all-white stuffed and corded quilts may not have originated in Provence. Certainly there were similar examples in nearby Sicily in the 15th century.[2] Provence was the "province of Rome" from the 2nd century BC, and the connections between southern France and Italy are very ancient.

The making of these quilts in Provence in the 17th century was not just an occasional event. It was a widely practiced folk art, developed to a high degree and well known as a regional tradition. Much quilted clothing was made, in particular petticoats and outer skirts called "cotillons." These provincial skirts were usually made of indiennes. On feast days, particularly that of Corpus Christi, the all-white bed quilts were hung outside the houses to honor the procession to the church.[3]

One of France's 19th century poets was Frederic Mistral, a native of Provence, who was awarded a Nobel prize in 1904. His lengthy poems were about the old days and simple folk of Provence. In a poem titled *Calendral* published in 1867, Mistral referred to the traditional white quiltings, calling them "divine work that recalls a meadow when frost embroiders in white all the leaves and branches."[4] In an earlier poem *Mireio* (1859), Mistral wrote:

A smart red petticoat she first prepares
Which she herself had quilted into squares,—
Of needlework a very masterpiece;
And round her slender waist she fastens this;
And over it another finer one
She draws;[5]

The fabric of these quilts was usually white silk or linen, although other colors were used, and woolen fabric as well. Cotton imported from India was also used early in Provence. Prints from India and, later, French "indiennes" were used also.

The corded quilts were made by using a special instrument called a "boutis." This was a thin, flexible rod around which a soft cord was wrapped. It was then inserted between the lines of quilting, held at the far end, and the boutis removed leaving the cord in place. Large pieces such as bedquilts and petticoats were quilted on large wooden frames.[6]

For 2500 years the major seaport of Provence has been Marseilles —a port of call for traders of many nations. The quilts of Provence inevitably found their way into the international trade—probably in the 17th century. When they arrived in England, they were referred to by their place of purchase—Marseilles quilts. They appear to have arrived in sufficient numbers for the name "Marseilles quilt" to be commonly understood in England to mean a whole-cloth stuffed or corded quilt. "Quilt" in England might mean either a bed-quilt or a petticoat. Beyond the bedquilts and petticoats, there was also exported from southern France a great deal of quilted silk yardage to be fashioned into petticoats, linings, waistcoats, and as the basis for embroideries.

An early reference to a Marseilles quilt in England is contained in two letters from Henry Purefoy to Anthony Baxter in London. Purefoy, on July 15, 1739, sent an order for a "neat white quilted calico petticoat for my Mother which must be a yard and four inches long." On August 5 he wrote again to say "I received all the things in the box and have returned you the Marseilles Quilt petticoat . . . It is so heavy my mother cannot wearing it."[7]

The early quilts that came to America came through English merchants, and appear to have lost the French designation on the voyage. They are much more likely to be referred to by their fabric. In some orders sent from Virginia to the London merchant John Norton, the following are included: Sept. 16, 1760—"a Redd Sarcenett Quilted Petticoat" and "2 bedd quilts" ordered by John Baylor; August 18, 1768—"several bundles of best quilt" [yardage] ordered by George Wythe; Sept. 25, 1771—"One green peeling [peelong] Satin quilted Petticoat for a tall Woman" ordered by Peter Lyons; and Jan. 31, 1772—"4 White Quilted Peeling Child Bed Basket & Pin Cushions well & safe Packed up or the Sattin will Mildue" ordered by Catherine Rathell, a shopkeeper in Williamsburg.[8]

England and France were still traditional rivals during this period. In America they competed for the fur-and-textile trade in Canada and along the whole length of the Mississippi. England was almost fully occupied with weaving. Her foreign trade depended heavily on the sales and shipment of cloth. The English weaving industry was characterized by doing the same thing over and over— very well and with a high degree of dependability. France also had important weaving centers. Her forte was in producing fancy fabrics, silks, brocades, ribbons, laces and very fine woolens.

In the first half of the 18th century, however, a number of new inventions were made in the weaving trade, and now innovation became a way to meet the competition. In England and France, and later in the young United States, great efforts were made to develop new techniques and to steal industrial secrets from the other countries. What could be patented in one country was no protection from its free use in another country.

In 1762 a patent for a new type of weaving was recorded in England by George Glasgow. It was "a method of weaving cloth in imitation of women's stiched stays." The drawings submitted showed the specifications for "weaving together two, three and four pieces of single cloth, so that they will appear as if stitched together."[9] On March 9 of 1763, Glasgow and Robert Elder jointly registered a patent for a "new method of weaving and quilting in the loom, in every method, fashion and figure, as well in imitation of the common manner of quilting, as of India, French and Marseilles quilting." The method specifies the need for a draw boy to pull up the many different shafts in the proper order to create the pattern.[10] The language used in this patent record tells us that Marseilles quilting was different from the "common Manner" of quilting, and that it was fully recognizeable in England by name.

A word about nomenclature. In the England of the 17th and 18th centuries, there is no evidence of a wide-spread hand-quilting tradition such as in Provence. Existing records suggest that quilting in England was a specialty rather than a commonality. The English were weavers. When they first imitated Marseilles quilts, they simply called the procedure "quilting in the loom" and the products "quilts." They have retained this usage and, even today, a particular kind of wool honeycomb blanket woven in Wales is called a Welsh quilt. American usage has followed British usage, especially among merchants and manufacturers. The hand-made quilts of Provence do not seem to have been called by their French title in America as they were in England. Therefore, in an American reference after 1800, a "Marseilles quilt" is confidently a loom-made bed spread. Now, in the United States, a distinction is made between an article made from two separate layers of cloth stitched together—with or without a batting—(a quilt) and a bedcover made on a loom (called either a coverlet, counterpane or bed spread). For American scholars the modern term for the type of bed spread to be considered here is "Marseilles spread."

The news of the "new method of quilting in the loom" traveled fairly rapidly. In 1765 the Georgia GAZETTE of Savannah published this item:

"London, February 7. The business of quilting bed-carpets and petticoats, which formerly the females engrossed, is now totally going into a different channel, the weavers in Spittalfields having struck upon a method of quilting in their looms, which is much cheaper and neater than any person with a needle can do."[11]

In 1776 in London, The Society for the Encouragement of Arts, Manufactures and Commerce published a book describing items contained in its Repository. Chapter XI is titled *Linen, Woolen, Silk and Cotton, Quilted in the Loom, in Imitation of Marseilles and Italian Quilting,* and in it the author remarked that "the advancement of the art of Quilting in the Loom is very extraordinary." The chapter ends: "N.B. Specimens of the different sorts of Quilting are preserved in the Society's Repository of Manufactures."[12]

Ten different weavers were named in the chapter as having received a premium from the Society for their work in the years 1762–1765. The two men who submitted the patent application in 1763 were not among the winners. It would appear that the method was already known by other weavers before the patent was applied for.

In 1783 the Society published its TRANSACTIONS, giving a summary of their rewards for the year. Included for the class of Manufactures was a total of 597 pounds awarded for "Quilting in the Loom, and spinning several sorts of Yarn." Also in a paragraph entitled "Quilting in the Loom," the compiler commented:

"When the proposition was first made in the Society, of offering a premium to encourage the making in the Loom, an imitation of that species of Needle-work, long known by the name of Marseilles Quilting, it was almost rejected as visionary and impossible; but the laudable spirit of enterprize, which has always distinguished this Society, determined them to publish the premium, and the consequence has justified the measure. This success animated them to continue their premiums, in hopes of further improvement, in which they were not disappointed. The manufacture is now so thoroughly established,

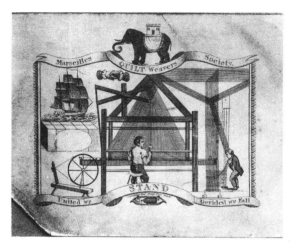

Fig. 2. *Marseilles Quilt Weavers Society card, circa 1875. IND. 22. Bolton Museum Archives. Courtesy Bolton Metropolitan Borough, Department of Education and Arts.*

and so extensive, being wrought in all the different materials of Linen, Woolen, Cotton, and Silk, that there are few persons of any rank, condition, or sex, in the kingdom, (and we may add, within the extent of British commerce, so greatly is it exported) who do not use it in some part of their clothing; so that we may safely say, if the whole fund and revenue of the Society had been given to obtain this one article of Trade, the national gain in return should be considered as very cheaply purchased."[13]

Despite the hyperbole in this paragraph, it is still clear that loom-made Marseilles quilting was greatly singled out for praise. In the brief twenty year period following the first premiums awarded, the new product had established an important place in the British family of fabrics. From the early frank imitations of the needle quilting of Provence, the English weavers were developing a whole *new family* of fabric construction quite different from the ancient English flat woolens. This new family was called by the name of "quiltings." The basic construction of quiltings consists of a double-cloth made on a drawloom so the two layers can be "stitched" together, and containing an unwoven stuffing layer.

The drawloom had been in use for the weaving of intricate patterns since at least early Christian time. If of large size, it required the help of one or more persons (known as drawboys) to pull predetermined warp yarns out of their ordinary position during the weaving. The sequence in which this was done determined the resulting pattern. By the 17th century the drawloom was well known throughout Europe, being used mostly for patterned silks.

Double-cloth is also an ancient technique. It was woven very early in China, and in Peru before the Christian era. Double-cloth can be woven on a very simple 4-heddle loom. If the two faces are of different yarns, they can be interchanged to form designs, as is done in Jacquard coverlets.

In quiltings, the two faces are not interchanged. The top face is constructed of finer yarns in a finer weave than the back face. The only interchange comes at the "stitches," where a single pick of yarn from the back comes to the front and holds the front face at that point. Such "stitch" picks can be arranged in *any* design. During the row-by-row weaving, the soft unspun filling layer is laid down and held in place by the "stitches."

What was new to the English weaving scene in the second half of the eighteenth century was the combination of double (or triple) cloth with the intricate patterning of the drawloom. This innovation, creating a three dimensional cloth, was a great departure from a smooth, continuous, flat surface—previously a hallmark of Britain's fine woolens. Introduced at a time of other new developments in spinning, weaving and the use of cotton in England, quilting in the loom combined with them in the production of cotton quiltings. Probably the English-French rivalry played its part. The English weavers could now make "Marseilles" quiltings faster than the women of Provence, and English merchants could market them readily through their superior trade routes.

These woven quiltings took many forms. Just as the needle-made quilts of France were made as often for clothing and furnishings as they were for bedding, so were the woven quiltings. Many new sorts of quiltings were developed using the ever finer and stronger cotton yarns. It is probably these new fabric variations rather than the bedcoverings alone that were so popular a manufacture as to warrant the high praise given them in 1793 by the Society for the Encourage-

ment of Arts, etc. In 1800 in the COMMERCIAL AND AGRICUL-
TURAL MAGAZINE of London, in a brief history of the Society the
author wrote: "The art of QUILTING IN THE LOOM was one of the
most generally useful of all those which, in the preparation of elegant
cloth, this Society's exertions gained to Britain."[14]

In a comprehensive study of British overseas trade, Elizabeth
Boody Schumpeter calculated the amounts of cotton textiles exported from Britain during the years 1697 through 1807. Compared
with the amount of exported woolens, cottons were a miniscule part
of the export trade until 1782 when they took a significant rise. In
every year after that, cotton exports increased, and in 1802 they outdistanced woolens in value to Britain.[15] The export of (undifferen-
tiated) cotton counterpanes is separately listed from 1798 when
almost 14,000 were shipped overseas. In the years following (to 1807
—the final year of the study) the numbers were fewer—rising to
more than 12,000 only in 1804, 1806, and 1807. Cotton "manufactures," which may be supposed to be quiltings and fancies, doubled
in the value of exports between 1799 and 1807, and far outdistanced
the value of counterpanes. In this same period the number and value
of printed cottons and linen-and-cotton also rose dramatically and
accounted for almost half of the total cotton exports.[16]

The quiltings were sold widely in America. Presumably they
would have been in greatest abundance on the eastern seaboard, but
they made their early way into the interior as well. Among early
mentions is one in the sales records of a Bowling Green, Kentucky
general store in 1806, when "1 yd Marseillez" was sold.[17] Another
"account of Goods Put in Red Store" (probably in Massachusetts)
lists "2½ yds Marsails at 9/" on the first of May 1806.[18] In 1808 in
St. Louis, J. Philipson's accounts show the sale of "¾ yds Marseills—
$2.50"—a rather high price for a fabric less than a yard wide.[19]
Although the spelling may have been as fancy as the fabrics, the
handed-down name "Marseilles" perhaps gave them the image of
being French and therefore, in American eyes, particularly
desireable.

Cotton "fancies"—meaning fabrics of complex structure—of this
early period were all made on the drawloom. As the major place of
their manufacture was Bolton, in Lancashire, they were also referred
to as "Bolton quiltings." Later weavers formed their own association

Figs. 3 & 4. Swatches from merchant's sample book, probably from Manchester (England) circa 1783. #G 1974-570. Courtesy of the Colonial Williamsburg Foundation.

Fig. 5. & 6. Swatches of "marcella" from Ackermann's REPOSITORY, July and August 1809. Negs. #82.505 and 83.137. Courtesy of Henry Francis du Pont Winterthur Museum Library: Collection of Rare Books.

called the Marseilles Quilt Weavers Society. Their card (Figure 2) illuminates the connection between the drawloom (complete with drawboy) and overseas commerce represented by the sailing vessel, with an Indian elephant probably representing the early source of cotton.

It would be nice to know what the very earliest quiltings looked like. Particularly those in the Repository of Manufactures of the Society of Arts. However, according to the curator-librarian of that institution, "the contents of the Society's Repository were dispersed in the 1850s" and "the specimens have not survived."[20] There is in the Colonial Williamsburg collections a sample book of about 1783 containing quiltings of that date. The sample book is almost certainly one made up as a catalogue by a merchant in Manchester, England.[21] It contains more than 500 samples of different cotton fabrics—plain, printed or fancy-woven. Two swatches of quiltings (Figures 3 and 4) exhibit simple designs of diamonds. The size of each swatch is approximately 1 x 1½ inches, thus the woven pattern is quite petite.

Samples of twenty-five years later can be found in Ackermann's REPOSITORY.[22] In each monthly issue of that periodical, Ackermann pasted in three or four swatches of fashionable fabrics. Four of these in 1809 were quiltings called "marcella"—a takeoff on Marseille—and were recommended for gentlemen's waistcoats. The woven designs are fine and small and are further embellished with printed designs. Close examination of these small swatches reveals the unwoven stuffing layer in these quiltings (Figures 5 and 6).

In the Archive of the Borough of Bolton, Lancashire, is an 1841 pattern book of James Hardcastle & Company, Ltd., Bolton, that contains samples of similar quiltings for vesting, with overprinted fine designs. Another book in the Bolton Museum includes undated samples (Figures 7, 8, 9 and 10) of a number of different kinds of quiltings traditionally made in Bolton.[23]

Some of these early "marseilles" fabrics have been used as foundation fabrics for quilts and unquilted applique coverlets. Dunton, in OLD QUILTS, recorded eight appliqued coverlets from the period 1820–30 in which the foundation fabric was marseilles quilting. The coverlets were attributed to the design of Achsah Goodwin Wilkins of Baltimore. Dunton carefully noted some of the details of the fabrics. Designs were recorded as: "a repeat pattern of diamonds;" "a diapered pattern of flat lozenges 14 x 20 mm. with separating bands 4 mm. wide;" "a diamond design 30 x 40 mm wide, or about twice the size of the diamonds of the marseilles" noted before; "marseilles of a different pattern;" "a rosebud design with a woven border;" and "a marseilles more elaborate in design . . . a braided or basket effect as though made with fancy ribbon." Dunton also noted that one of the eight coverlets was constructed on a marseilles base of two strips of four foot width, and three others on four strips ranging in width from 27½ to 30 inches.[24]

Existing early drawloom-made Marseilles spreads of full size are difficult to date with any confidence. They are widely scattered and, being difficult to photograph, are hard to study on a comparative basis. They are easily recognizeable — all being made of white cotton, having a fine-woven face cloth, a coarser back cloth, and a heavy unspun cotton roving as a stuffing layer. Many have worn areas where the roving is readily seen (Figure 11).

The old spreads are quite large and without a center seam. One such spread at Connor Prairie Pioneer Settlement measures 105 x 114 inches,[25] while another at the DAR Museum measures 105 x 104 inches.[26] Old Sturbridge Village collections include a Marseilles spread measuring 100 x 109 inches[27] (Figure 12) and a mid-19th century example of smaller size is in the collections of the M.H. de Young Memorial Museum[28] (Figure 13). Most Marseilles spreads have a round or oval central medallion with various surrounding designs and borders.

It is difficult also to determine which of the spreads may have been made in America. An effort was made in Fredericksburg, Virginia in 1777 to establish a manufactory which was "capable of manufacturing . . . drawboys, quiltings, figured work of all sorts"[29] and also in Beverly, Massachusetts in 1788, where a Mr. Leonard and Mr. Somers, who were setting up a carding and spinning mill, "understood the making and finishing of velverets, corduroys, jeans, fustians, denims, marseilles quiltings, dimity and muslins."[30] A newspaper advertisement in Baltimore in 1792 offered the publication entitled THE WEAVER'S DRAUGHT-BOOK AND CLOTHIER'S ASSISTANT, which included drafts for "Diapers, Counterpanes, . . . Mock-Marseilles," and other fabrics.[31] There is no indication that

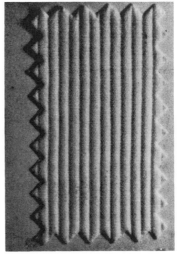

Fig. 7. Marseilles Quilt. "Home trade and shipped to the Colonies."

Fig. 8. Piqué. "Home trade and shipped all over the world."

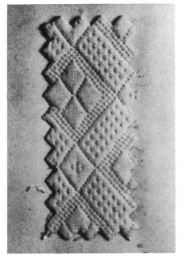

Fig. 9. Toilet. "Used as quilts and table covers."

Fig. 10. Mitcheline or Patent Satin Quilt. "Used for quilts or counterpanes. Home trade and the Colonies."

From W. Hough, COTTON FABRICS, Bolton Museum Archives, Bolton Metropolitan Borough, Department of Education and Arts.

Fig. 11. Detail, reverse of Marseilles spread. #5255, Gift of Mrs. C. Edward Murray, The Daughters of the American Revolution Museum. Photo by Gloria Allen.

Fig. 12. Detail, corner of Marseilles spread, circa 1810–40. #26.10.127, Old Sturbridge Village. Photo by Henry E. Peach.

Fig. 13. Marseilles spread, circa 1860. #67.19, Gift of Mrs. R.R. Newell, The Fine Arts Museums of San Francisco.

any Marseilles spreads were actually produced by those early enterprises.

At some time, production did begin in the United States. The catalogue of the Great National Fair of 1844, held at Washington, includes as part of entry No. 301 from Yates & Canby, Baltimore: "From Joseph Haslam, Patterson, N.J., 1 bale specimens counter-panes and quilts prices from $1.50 to $3.00 each" and as entry

No. 440: "Lancaster Mills, Lancaster, Mass., 3 cases quilts, different sizes.;[32] By this date, however, the jacquard loom was certainly a part of the picture.

Between 1810 and 1820 the jacquard mechanism had begun replacing the drawboys of England. The process was adopted slowly, partly because of the great height of the mechanisms. Placed on top of the already large hand looms, they required a room with a twelve-foot ceiling—not readily available to many weavers. The mechanisms gradually improved and diminished in size, and weavers began to use them for their convenience and versatility.

As the 19th century progressed, the character of Marseilles spreads changed. They gradually became thinner, flatter, lighter in weight and with more elaborate and smaller patterning. They no longer looked at all like the quilts of Provence. Some even lost their stuffing layer, reverting to a simple double weave though retaining the name Marseilles. As recently as 1902 in the Sears, Roebuck and Company catalogue and 1916 in a wholesale catalogue issued by J.H. Dunham & Co., New York, "Marseilles quilts" were included with other bedspreads. Oddly enough, some of the 20th century Marseilles spreads again tried to look like quilts, but now it was American quilts they imitated (Figure 14).

Other bed spreads and fabrics belong in this woven family of discontinuous surface textiles. Not all have a fully hidden third layer, and many were developed after the jacquard loom fully replaced the drawloom. Although not inspired directly by true quilts, they owe their idea to the needle-worked Provencal quilts and are still called by the general name of "quiltings." Some of the 19th and 20th century variations are named: Mitcheline, patent satin, matelasé, Alhambra quiltings, piqué, honeycombs, Bedford cord, and toileting or toilets. Loom-made double cloth quiltings went out of fashion after 1925. References in most textbooks and glossaries after that time—if they include them at all—refer to them as "obsolete" curiosities.

Two more British patents are of interest in this development. Oddly enough, 97 years after the first patents were recorded in England, and long after the weaving technique was fully understood and utilized, quilting in the loom appears again in the patent records. On January 6, 1859, James Kirkman and Isaac Grundy

Fig. 14. Early 20th century "Marseilles spread." Double cloth, no filling. Collection of author.

stated in their description: "This invention is applicable to the manufacture of fabrics known as Bolton or Marseilles quilts, or others of like texture and materials." On January 7th Edwin Heywood offered a patent statement that is worth quoting at some length.

> "The improvements relate to the production of a peculiar description of double fabrics united in the weaving at parts, and enclosing between them thread or yarn as stuffing; such fabric being adapted to be used for skirts, ladies petticoats, the lining of coats and other garments, and for other uses in imitation of where two fabrics are united by stitching in various forms, and enclosing wool or other matter as padding.... The imitation of or resemblance to stitching is obtained by the weft and warps in the lines or forms desired, being caused to unite the two fabrics, and at the same time hold in position the thick or soft threads between them. Such uniting threads may be of silk or other material, different from that used for the general surface of the fabric in order that as it appears on the surface of the fabric produced it may represent stitching or other sewing."[33]

Thus, in 1859, recognition was again paid to the quilters of France of three centuries ago.

Notes and References:

1. Henri Algoud, "Toiles ornées au boutis et Indiennes de Provence," LA SOIERIE DE LYON, Lyon, 1926, pp. 636–642. Courtesy Musée des Tissus, Lyon, France.

2. Two corded and stuffed quilts from Sicily, c. 1395, are in the collections of the Victoria and Albert Museum, London, and the Bargello, Florence. Photographs and discussion in: Averil Colby, QUILTING, Batsford, London, 1972, pp. 13–16.

3. Algoud, p. 637.

4. Algoud, p. 637.

5. "Mireio" is the poem for which Frederic Mistral was given a Nobel prize. It is published (in English) in NOBEL PRIZE LIBRARY, Vol. 15, Helvetica Press, New York, 1971, p. 188.

6. Algoud, pp. 636, 638.

7. Janet Arnold, PATTERNS OF FASHION, Wace & Co., London, 1964, p. 4. Quoted in: Mildred B. Lanier, "Marseilles Quiltings of the 18th and 19th Centuries," Bulletin de Liaison du CIETA, #47/48, 1978, p. 74. Courtesy Musée des Tissus.

8. Frances Norton Mason, JOHN NORTON AND SONS: MERCHANTS OF LONDON AND VIRGINIA, David & Charles, Newton Abbot, 1937, pp. 10, 58, 190, 218.

9. B. Woodcroft, ed., PATENTS FOR INVENTIONS: ABRIDGMENTS OF SPECIFICATIONS RELATING TO WEAVING, The Great Seal Patent Office, London, 1861, pp. 8–9.

10. Woodcroft, p. 9.

11. GEORGIA GAZETTE, Savannah, 6 June 1765. Courtesy Museum of Early Southern Decorative Arts, Winston-Salem, NC.

12. Alexander Mabyn Bailey, THE ADVANCEMENT OF ARTS, MANUFACTURES, AND COMMERCE, Society for the Encouragement of Arts, etc., London, 1776, p. 130. Courtesy Merrimack Valley Textile Museum Library, North Andover, MA. A curious comment in this chapter:

    "This new and useful manufacture was invented by a poor obscure journeyman weaver, whose views, at first, extended no farther than to make a small quantity of it for the use of his wife and children; but, before it was made into garments for them, it was shewn, as a matter of curiosity, to a gentlewoman, who ... mentioned it to the author of this book; and he...with great difficulty, found out the ingenious inventor;"

The author, however, does not name the ingenious inventor!

13. TRANSACTIONS OF THE SOCIETY, Society of Arts, London, 1783, p. 25. Courtesy MVTM Library.
14. "History of the Society of Arts, etc.," COMMERCIAL & AGRICULTURAL MAGAZINE, London, February 1800, p. 109. Courtesy MVTM Library.
15. Elizabeth Boody Schumpeter, ENGLISH OVERSEAS TRADE STATISTICS 1697–1808, Clarendon Press, Oxford, 1960, p. 12.
16. Schumpeter, "Table XI: Quantities and Values of the Principal British Exports of Textile Goods (excluding Woolens) for the Years 1772–1807," pp. 31–34. Courtesy MVTM Library.
17. Ms. SC. 294 BSB: day book, Gatewood and Chapline, merchants, Bowling Green, Kentucky, p. 15. Account of Robert Magness. Manuscript Division, Kentucky Library, Western Kentucky University, Bowling Green, KY.
18. Ms. 1964.61: "an account of Goods Put in Red Store," Old Sturbridge Village Research Library, Sturbridge, MA.
19. Day book, "Joseph Philipson Merchant St. Louis 1807," p. 42. Account of Alexr. McNair, March 29, 1808. St. Louis Mercantile Library, St. Louis, MO.
20. Letter: D.G.C. Allan, Curator-Librarian, The Royal Society of Arts, London, 26 February 1982; to author.
21. #G 1974-570: Swatch book circa 1783, "#50," Textiles Department, Colonial Williamsburg Foundation, Williamsburg, VA.
22. R. Ackermann, REPOSITORY OF ARTS, LITERATURE, COMMERCE, MANUFACTURES, FASHIONS AND POLITICS, London, 1809, issues for May, June, August and September. Courtesy Winterthur Research Library, Winterthur, DE. Printed descriptions read:

May—"No. 4 is called printed India rib. It is a species of marcella, and is, at this moment, a very fashionable article for gentlemen's waistcoats."

July—"No. 4. This chintz, or shawl pattern marcella, 2/4 wide, is a truly elegant and fashionable article for gentlemen's waistcoats."

August—"No. 4 is a printed diamond marcella quilting, for gentle men's waistcoats. On this article there is little need of comment, except to call the attention of our readers to the peculiar delicacy of the printed stripe, which has perhaps rendered it so universal a favorite with men of high fashion. It is ¾ wide, and from 9s. to 10s. per yard." September — "No. 4 is a unique article in silk striped quilting, combining much delicacy and utility; and which the inventor, after much labour, and considerable expence, has brought to its present high state of perfection, at his manufactory in the north of England."

23. W. Hough, COTTON FABRICS, Typed manuscript with swatches, 1922. Archives, Bolton Museum, Bolton, Lancashire.

24. William Rush Dunton, Jr., OLD QUILTS, privately published, Baltimore, 1946, pp. 184–98.

25. CPM-1134. Marseilles spread circa 1825, 105″ x 114″. Connor Prairie Pioneer Settlement, Connorsville, IN.

26. 5255. Marseilles spread, 105″ x 104″. Gift of Mrs. C. Edward Murray. Daughters of the American Revolution Museum, Washington, DC.

27. 26.10.127. Marseilles spread circa 1810–1840, 100″ x 109″. Old Sturbridge Village, Sturbridge, MA.

28. 67.19. Marseilles spread circa 1860, 86¼″ x 77½″. M.H. de Young Memorial Museum, San Francisco, CA.

29. Advertisement, VIRGINIA GAZETTE, Fredericksburg, Jan. 1, 1777. Quoted in: Lanier, "Marseilles Quiltings," p. 76.

30. Salem MERCURY, (May?) 1788. Quoted in: Perry Walton, THE STORY OF TEXTILES, Tudor, New York, 1925, p. 154.

31. The MARYLAND JOURNAL AND BALTIMORE ADVERTISER, 16 March 1792. Courtesy MESDA. The booklet advertised, THE WEAVERS DRAFT BOOK AND CLOTHIERS ASSISTANT, by John Hargrove, is the earliest draft book known to be printed in America. It was republished in facsimile by the American Antiquarian Society in 1979. None of Hargrove's 52 drafts is called Mock-Marseilles in his book, although he did include three different birds-eye designs and a "Deception Diaper."

32. THE NATIONAL MAGAZINE & INDUSTRIAL RECORD, Vol. 1, New York, 1845, p. 161.

33. Woodcroft, PATENTS FOR INVENTIONS, pp. 955, 957.

Index

The American Quilt Study Group is a nonprofit organization devoted to uncovering and disseminating the history of quiltmaking as a significant part of American art and culture. AQSG encourages and supports research on quilts, quiltmaking, quiltmakers, and the textiles and materials of quilts. Membership and participation are open to all interested persons. For further information, contact the American Quilt Study Group, 660 Mission Street, Suite 400, San Francisco, CA 94105.

AQSG

- sponsors an exciting seminar each year
- publishes an annual volume, *Uncoverings*
- maintains a library and research facility
- produces a series of *Technical Guides*
- publishes the newsletter, *Blanket Statements*
- offers research grants and scholarships
- serves as an information center

AMERICAN QUILT STUDY GROUP

AQSG's goal is to develop a responsible and accurate body of information about quilts and their makers. A reliable history of quiltmaking provides insights into the lives and times of quiltmakers, and connects women with their heritage and their place in creative art.

We welcome all persons interested in the history of quiltmaking. Our members include quilt lovers, traditional and contemporary quilt artists, dealers, collectors, researchers, authors, museum curators, students of women's studies, and folklorists.

Discover the thrill of dating your grandmother's quilt from its fabrics, or of tracing the great quilt you bought at a flea market back to its maker.

Membership in AQSG opens the door to a wonderful network of people who are passionate about quilts and whose interests range across every level of quilting.

The American Quilt Study Group is dedicated to preserving the story of quiltmaking – past, present, and future. We invite you to join our ranks!

> "No other group has done as much as AQSG to document and preserve America's quilt history. If you only support one quilt organization, this is the one!"
> —Julie Silber, Quilt Curator, Lecturer

> "The American Quilt Study Group has maintained its commitment to sound and significant quilt scholarship. Its annual journal, Uncoverings, is a must for those seriously interested in the subject."
> —Jonathan Holstein, Quilt Historian, Author

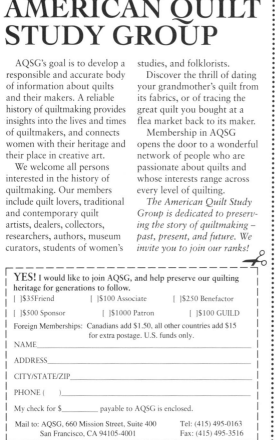